Twelve Kids, One Bathroom, and a Milk Bottle

Pat UPTON Stamm

iUniverse, Inc.
New York Bloomington

Twelve Kids, One Bathroom, and a Milk Bottle

iUniverse books may be ordered through booksellers or by contacting:

iUniverse
1663 Liberty Drive
Bloomington, IN 47403
www.iuniverse.com
1-800-Authors (1-800-288-4677)

ISBN: 978-1-4401-8874-9 (pbk)
ISBN: 978-1-4401-8876-3 (cloth)
ISBN: 978-1-4401-8875-6 (ebk)

Printed in the United States of America

iUniverse rev. date: 11/5/2009

To my parents, George and Elvira Upton, who filled my heart with the love, pride and memories that are within this book.

To my husband and best friend, Bill Stamm, who has been totally supportive of my writing this book.

Introduction

My mother would call out the front window, "Georgie, Dolores, Patty, Reenie, Jeri, Lorraine, Raymond, Eddie, Dennis, Robert, Tommy, Adrianne, come on up—dinner is on the table!" Needless to say, we stampeded up the stairs, ran into the kitchen, and there was dinner - on the table! We were so poor that we didn't have any dishes! It's not true, but it's a story I made up (one of many) when Sr. Anne Louise, my high school steno teacher, said she had five minutes left before the bell. She would ask me, on these rare occasions of spare time, to tell the class about various events in my exceptionally large family.

Anyone who meets me for the first time will know within five minutes that I am the third of twelve children and am very proud of that distinction. We were not wealthy financially. We were quite average in the fact that a lot of large families existed in those days, and everyone struggled to survive, not just us. But we were rich in the fortune of having two hardworking parents whose love for each other surrounded and protected us. We were fortified by their love to stand up against injustices in the world and were always told that "nothing is impossible" and we could "be" anything we wanted as long as we worked hard for it. We were shown by the example of my Irish Catholic father and my German Lutheran mother, who were up against the world from the start.

Let me remind anyone reading this that I am only *one* of the twelve, and will be sharing *my* memories. Each of us - me and all my brothers and sisters – is unique and has a variety of feelings and recollections, depending on when we were born. Everything I write is said with the deepest love and respect for my family.

Chapter 1

It all started when this tall, thin, good-looking Irishman with black hair and hazel eyes hurriedly ran into the bakery in Brooklyn to get change for $1. He didn't buy anything but was met by the strikingly beautiful, 5' 2" blue-eyed salesgirl with golden brown hair. He thanked her for the change and promised he'd be back to take her to a movie. He kept his promise. Little did they know, George Upton and Elvira Wolf, that they were entering the path of a lifetime together.

George Thomas Upton (our father), born October 29, 1911, was the son of Edward Patrick Upton and Mary Ann (Boyle) Upton, the parents of eleven children—Bernard, Marion, Edward, John, George, Thomas, Raymond, Joseph, Dorothy, Francis, and Anna. Our grandfather, Edward Patrick Upton, worked as a blacksmith and tool and die maker, creating tools for making gravestones across the street from Cypress Hills Cemetery.

My father used to tell us stories of how when they all went to church, they had to go in shifts. Back then boys wore knickers, a kind of baggy pants gathered below the knees, with accompanying knee-high socks. They didn't have enough for everyone, so whoever went to church first ran home quick so the next brother could dress in the same clothes and go to Mass. The socks were pretty worn and had holes in them, so they filled in the holes with shoe polish. I saw nothing wrong with wearing "holey" socks to Mass. Most of my Upton aunts and uncles spoke with a very Brooklynese accent. Instead of "boiling" water, they "berled" it, and they were careful not to "serl" their clothes.

Elvira Wanda Victoria (Wolf) Upton (our mother), born July 12, 1914, was the daughter of Erich Paul Florian Wolf and Wanda

Victoria Stephania (Richter) Wolf, the parents of seven children, Erich, Elvira, Helmuth (Pinky), Herbert, Vincent (Bumpsy), Howard, and Olga. Olga died before she was 2, of what we never knew, so my mother was the only girl. Mom told us that Grandma would stay up all hours of the night sewing, using old clothing, turning them inside out to make outfits for the children, since times were tough. Grandma and Grandpa Wolf owned a German deli, and Mom's spare time and days off from school were spent helping to cook the roasted meats and make the potato and macaroni salads to be sold. Grandma's and Mom's potato salads were the best!

Grandma Wolf, born February 5, 1890, ventured to America by herself at the age of 20. Grandma, of German descent, was from Lodz (pronounced Wooch), Prussia, and I'm sure it was quite a journey alone. I always figured that she came over as a steerage passenger, which was for the poorest and lowest class, who tumbled around sickly from the rough seas. I was wrong. Fraulein Wanda Richter traveled first class. I have the passenger list and menus from the *Roon*, the ship she sailed on, which departed from Bremen, Germany in November 1910. She could speak, read, and write English, German, Polish, Hebrew, Yiddish, and more. Grandma was short – barely five feet tall - zoftig in stature, always a lady in manner, and even when food shopping wore her hat, gloves and scarf. She was helpful and caring but not overly affectionate by nature. She was well organized and certainly a take-charge person. She had to be since Grandpa was a bit impish and she had to call the shots to keep his mind on business.

Grandma and Grandpa Wolf met at a dance in Manhattan. I can picture the women then standing on one side of the dance hall in long, full skirts, tightly pulled sashes to show a slim waist, and high-necked, long-sleeved blouses, topped off with a severe hairdo wrapped in a bun. The men in their stately suits, laced-up high shoes, and very appropriate pocket watches, stood tall and proper on the other side of the room, discreetly eyeing the ladies. The men would cross the room, bow slightly, and request a dance with their lady of choice. After they met, Grandpa had difficulty finding Fraulein Richter. He kept searching for "Peenee" Street instead of Pine Street, where she lived. They were married in Hoboken, New Jersey, on January 16, 1912. Erich and Wanda Wolf received their Certificate of Naturalization on June 1, 1921, when Mom was 7 years old.

Grandpa Wolf, born August 3, 1887, in Hanover, Germany, was a violinist and played in the Philharmonic in Germany before coming to America. I never saw or heard him play, but Grandma showed me the Stradivarius violin he owned. Rumor has it that Grandpa defiantly deserted the German Army and ventured to America. As a young man Grandpa had a head full of red hair, but I have memories of a short, stout, balding man with a pretty bare head on top. Once in America, he played his violin at the New York Philharmonic and various social halls in New York City. His being a musician is the reason my mother's family and some of us were and still are "night owls." Playing his violin late into the night, Grandpa wasn't ready to sleep after work. Once he came to our house at three in the morning, rang the bell, and the lady downstairs heard him and started screaming "Black Hand! Black Hand!" (Black Hand was a notorious gang of hoodlums at the time.) Grandpa and my mother's brothers thought nothing of coming to visit late at night, like it was normal. They usually brought beer in cardboard containers, and Mom would put out salads, cold cuts, and coffee and cake. Mom was a coffee lover, and the aroma of fresh-percolated brew always filled the air. Nobody got drunk; they just sat around and ate, smoked, and talked like it was two in the afternoon. Mom maintained her night owl hours all her life.

While the country was still in the grips of the financial disaster of the Great Depression of 1929, George Upton and Elvira Wolf were married on June 28, 1936, at Our Lady of Lourdes Church in Brooklyn, with John Robertson and Paula Langerbin in attendance. At the time, this "mixed marriage" of a Catholic and a Lutheran was not accepted by either religion and was frowned upon by both families—the Uptons and the Wolfs. In order for the marriage to be recognized by the Catholic Church, my mother had to sign papers vowing she would raise any children of the union in the Catholic faith. Because of the "embarrassing" interfaith marriage, the wedding took place in the rectory of Our Lady of Lourdes Church because two people of different faiths could not be married at the altar. I often jest that my parents probably wore dark clothing, hoods over their heads, and had to marry under darkness of night. In spite of all the nonsense from the Catholic Church, Mom lived up to her promise to raise us Catholic—100%. My parents lived in Brooklyn when their first child, George Upton, Jr. was born on February 5, 1937. I've seen baby pictures of my brother George, and he was a cutey! I heard Mom was concerned that his ears weren't flat, so she put tape on them to hold them down and covered them with a tight bonnet. Any time a new baby was born in the family, Mom always had a fetish about flat ears. George's black hair and brown eyes were the features of the Irish Upton family, and I'm sure he was the little king.

On June 12, 1938, my sister Dolores was born—blonde, blue-eyed, and beautiful! She was a delight to the German side of the family. Dolores ended up with the nickname "La La" because

George had difficulty pronouncing her name. I've seen pictures of Dolores taken before I was born, and she was a beauty with golden ringlets and piercing blue eyes, and she was always dressed so nice. Both George and Dolores were born while my father's parents were still alive. Our paternal grandparents, Edward and Mary (Boyle) Upton, lived on Marion Street in Brooklyn. I never knew my father's parents, but Mom always said that my grandmother died so young - 43 - because of all those stairs she had to climb in that big house on Marion Street. My brother George attended the in-home wake for Grandpa Upton in 1944. That's how funerals were done then. Mom and Dad moved to Queens, and I often heard Mom say she didn't want to live in Brooklyn too close to the Uptons, who drank too much. In some cases, that proved to be true.

On January 16, 1942, right after the start of World War II, I, Patricia (Patty), was born in Queens General Hospital. I was blonde, blue-eyed, and very chubby. Mom told me I was so fat my first year that they couldn't find a snowsuit big enough for me, but most likely it was due to lack of money. Times were tough for everyone. Lives were changed due to the concentration on the war effort. All eligible men were drafted into the service, but Dad wasn't since he had flat feet. Dad worked as a plater and polisher at West Chemical Company in Long Island City but worked at Brewster Aircraft during the war.

I found out years later that Mom had tuberculosis when she carried me. Tuberculosis was quite prevalent in those years and the cause of a lot of deaths. I understand Mom was in and out of the Queens General Hospital/Tri-borough Solarium, and I was taken care of by Grandma Wolf and others from my mother's family. I recently learned that George and Dolores spent time in the Otillie Home in Jamaica while Mom was hospitalized. The doctors deflated one of Mom's lungs to rid her of the disease, and she lived the rest of her life with only one functioning lung. I have letters that my father wrote to my mother when she was in the hospital with TB. They are heart-wrenching and tender, written in pencil by a man whose heart was broken without his sweetheart beside him. In one letter, my father apologized for not visiting one night because he didn't have the nickel for the bus. Elvira—his Vera, his sweetheart—was his life.

Before you knew it, George and Vera were together again, and on February 10, 1943, a new playmate was born—blonde, blue-eyed, cuddly Maureen (Reenie)! She was smaller and more petite at birth than us ten-pounders. Almost two years later, on January 17, 1945, another adorable sister was born; dark-haired, brown-eyed Jerilynne (Jeri)! When Jeri was born, she had a "raspberry"-looking birthmark on her neck, near her collarbone. It wasn't dangerous or life threatening but needed to be removed. Mom took all of us with her on two buses to Queens General Hospital, where the doctors applied dry ice to baby Jeri's neck to eradicate the birthmark. It seemed only to be a one-minute application each visit, but it worked. Daddy always called Jeri his princess. I figured my father was thrilled, after having three blonde, blue-eyed girls, to finally have a daughter who looked like his side of the family! On June 6, 1946, another precious sister was born, brown-haired, brown-eyed Lorraine! To this day we kid her about the "666"—the sixth child, born the sixth day of the sixth month, in 1946! She's been a good sport about being tagged the "little devil." I wonder if George was starting to feel outnumbered by having five sisters. As we got older, we used to tease him with "Georgie Peorgie, pudding and pie, kissed the girls and made them cry."

Chapter 2

My first recollection of where we lived starts in Richmond Hill, Queens, on 117th Street, just south of Jerome (101st) Avenue. It was the upstairs apartment in a semi-attached two-family stucco house. Two cement steps led to a wood-floored porch, where the baby carriage was kept. The entrance door opened into a small vestibule with in-the-wall mailboxes, and another door led into the hall, which went back to the basement stairs. Just ahead were the stairs to our apartment. You entered the living room, and straight ahead was a bathroom with a black-and-white tiled floor and a tub on legs. (There was no shower.) To the right of the bathroom was an eat-in kitchen with a big hot water heater, which was so cozy to sit by in the winter. From the living room to the front of the apartment were three bedrooms, an alcove, and an unheated, screened-in porch overlooking the street. The front bedroom was for Mom and Dad and was where the crib was kept for the baby. The alcove was George's room, where he loved to read comic books and anything he could get his hands on, and he hid under the blankets with a flashlight to do so. Mom said that's why he wore glasses so young. There were shades and plastic curtains covering all the windows. As the family kept growing, *everything* became a bedroom!

The landlord was Mr. White, a very nice man who came once a month to collect the rent. Mom was especially sure that everything was in order when he came. When we heard Mr. White coming up the stairs, we all took our positions on the couch, covering up any holes and tears. After all, we didn't want the landlord to think we couldn't afford to live there! The couch was also used to "crease" Dad's and George's pants. Mom laid the pants under the cushions, and we all sat on top, hoping the weight of us sitting on it would maintain a crease. It worked!

I didn't really understand the occasion for it, but I recall being on the front screened-in porch when there was a huge block party taking place. Looking down with our dog Lucky, a mixed terrier I got for my third birthday, I saw everyone dancing, drinking, and being very happy. There were a lot of soldiers and sailors in uniform, and the street was mobbed and alive with celebration. I found out eventually that World War II had just ended in a great victory for America. (How was I to know? It was 1945, and I was only 3 ½.) Years later Mom told us how difficult it was for her brothers to fight against German soldiers during the war, sometimes feeling they could be shooting at their own cousins.

One of the best things about living on 117th Street was when we looked out the bathroom and kitchen windows and saw Daddy coming home from work. He took the bus on Lefferts Boulevard to the Eighth Avenue subway in Kew Gardens to get to and from his job at West Chemical Company in Long Island City. West Chemical was known for its CN pine cleaners, and also made Kotex, which was, in time, an advantage for the father of five daughters. When we spotted Daddy from the back windows, we'd wave and he would wave back, and we happily ran to the top of the stairs to await his smiling face. He always greeted his sweetheart Vera with a hug and a kiss and picked each of us up in his big, strong arms for the same.

When I was 5 years old I had my tonsils out at Mary Immaculate Hospital in Jamaica. It was a creepy experience. Whoever was pushing me on a moving bed (gurney) didn't say anything as we went down the halls through swinging doors. I was left alone in the hallway and was afraid I would roll through nearby swinging doors and never be found again! In those days, ether was the anesthetic that was used, and it smelled horrible and made you sick. When I woke up in a very dark room, a nurse gave me some Jell-O. The nurse turned out to be my Aunt Julie Upton, who was married to my father's brother Raymond at the time. When my parents came to take me home, I was all bundled up in Daddy's arms as we stood in front of the hospital while he hailed a taxicab. When we got in, my father said, "Hey, Mac, 117th and Jerome." I felt so safe and secure thinking my father knew the cab driver. Whether we took the train, bus, or taxi, or stopped to buy something, my father called everyone "Joe," "Mac," or "Harry," and I just figured my daddy knew everybody in the whole wide world! Boy, was I lucky!

When Dad worked in the West Chemical factory, he was an avid supporter and fighter for the unions. The pay was low, the work was hard, and benefits were nil. Paid sick days were unheard of. One time my father was hospitalized with pleurisy. We were crying when the ambulance drivers carried him out on a stretcher as all the neighbors watched. These were hard times for Mom and Dad in many ways; no work—no pay. My father continued to fight for unionization and eventually became a union representative. Through strikes, walk-outs, and perseverance, wages were raised and some benefits finally included. A sense of deserved fairness gave the factory workers more pride in their labor.

Mom and most women then wore housedresses every day. They were simple cotton dresses, usually buttoned down the front with a belt. Mom wore it as we kids all lay down with her to take a daily nap. We rested quietly while Mom put one arm across her eyes to block out the light, and my sisters and I laid our heads on the other arm, which was extended for us to do so. I liked to quietly look at Mom's beautiful face. I think the daily naps were more for the benefit of Mom, who was tired still from her bout with TB and of course childbearing. Her deflated lung became calcified as time passed, but *never* did you hear a word of complaint.

Mom was an excellent housekeeper, and we were all taught at a very young age to do our chores. And if something wasn't done right, it had to be done over again—like when I was washing the bathroom floor on hands and knees.

Mom: "You missed the corner."

Me: "I'll get the corner, Mom."

Mom: "Yes you will—when you do the whole floor over again!"

Believe me, we all learned to *do it right the first time!* We were all taught at a young age to make our beds, clean and dust the house, sweep and mop, wash the floors, wash and dry the dishes, clean the bathrooms, hang clothes out to dry, and iron. There were no steam irons then. We used to sprinkle each article of clothing with water first, then roll it up tight, so the dampness would seep through, making it easier to get rid of the wrinkles. We even ironed my father's undershirts, boxer shorts, and handkerchiefs. We all used handkerchiefs that were washed and ironed. Mom thought tissues were wasteful. Why buy something that had to be thrown away when handkerchiefs could be used over and over? Waste not, want not! Do not waste money! Every penny, nickel, and dime was saved or spent carefully.

Friday was the big cleaning day! We moved all the furniture to be sure to clean underneath everything. The linoleum covering the kitchen and living room floors was washed *and* waxed. Friday was when we also swept and scrubbed the vestibule, stairs, and hall leading into our apartment. But nobody—*none of us*—was allowed near Mom's stove. She took care of the cooking, her own little domain. I am thankful to this day for having a mother who taught us all so well to be good housekeepers.

When we were growing up, we didn't have a car or a telephone. We walked or bicycled everywhere we had to go, or took the bus or train. We went for our medical check-ups and shots at a clinic that was located on 116th Street just south of Jamaica Avenue. It was a walk we took all the time to accompany whoever was the new baby to be weighed, checked by the doctor, and receive whatever shots were necessary. Each child had a cubby space. Mom proudly undressed and played with her chubby little one for all to see what a beautiful, well-fed baby she had. There was also a record book she kept for each of us to keep track of our vaccinations—and to brag always about her strong, healthy babies. Mom did her part at home too, as each day we lined up for our dose of cod liver oil. *Yuck!* When one of us got the measles, mumps, or chicken pox, Mom made sure we played together so all of us would catch it and get it over with once and for all!

Richmond Hill is in Queens County, New York City, and in the '40s and '50s was considered the suburban part of the city. The population was a mixture of mostly Irish, German, and Italian families, many of which moved to Queens from Manhattan or Brooklyn because of the clean, country-like atmosphere that was conducive to raising a family. Richmond Hill was a middle-class neighborhood between Idlewild (now Kennedy) and LaGuardia Airports. The roaring of the overhead planes were daily sounds. There were many bus lines, two elevated trains, and easy access to most parts of the city. As I got older and the family grew, I thought, "Aha! Mom and Dad moved here so when we got old enough to move out, there would be plenty of transportation for us to do so!"

Taking buses in earlier days was an experience. You'd pay

your nickel fare and if necessary got a free transfer to another bus to reach your destination. Children 5 and under rode for free. Uncle Tom Upton, Dad's brother, was a cigar-smoking, New York City bus driver. He was a lot like my father in looks and humor and used to keep us in stitches with stories about his job. He said people must have thought he was blind and stupid when they'd get on the bus and swear the six-foot child with them was only 5 years old! He was good natured and would let it slide, knowing times were tough. Many times on the bus Mom didn't pay for her "exceptionally tall" 6, 7, 8 or 9-year-olds. A nickel was precious and well worth saving.

The street we lived on in Richmond Hill—117th—was a nice, tree-lined, one-way street between Jerome (101st) and 103rd Avenues. On the corner of Jerome Avenue was a German deli where there was always a display of six pretty faces of girls strung across from wall to wall, each vying for the title of "Miss Rheingold", a popular beer then. As young as I was, I always stopped in to cast a vote for the one I thought was prettiest. Next to the deli was a candy store where you could buy penny candy and a mellow-roll for 10¢, which was a special treat. On the opposite corner of Jerome Avenue was an empty lot, which was great for playing tag and hide and seek. Next to the lots, as we called it, was an original old diner that looked like an old, discarded railroad car. We didn't eat there, but we used to watch from the back window as the diner employees took live chickens out back and slaughtered them, feathers blowing in the wind. In the winter snow it was a bloody mess and looked like the scene of a massacre. If "fresh chicken" was advertised, it wasn't a lie! Eventually the diner was knocked down, the lots cleared, and a post office was built on the property. It was something to watch it emerge. Our house was behind it.

Being it was a two-family house, Mom and the lady downstairs from us often had arguments over use of the backyard. Mrs. M, a tall, husky woman, insisted it was only for her children's use, and Mom, much shorter and slighter of build, said it was for her children as well. Mom, though shy by nature, was feisty and not one to be pushed around. After a few yelling matches, we all had fun playing in the yard. Mrs. Upton refused to back off or be intimidated easily. She literally fought for what was right and fair and taught us to do the same.

Every night Mom and Dad had coffee while they read the newspapers. One time I heard them discussing a newspaper article about new homes being built in this place called Levittown. They only cost $6,000 and were affordable houses built for the servicemen returning from the war. They discussed the possibility of buying a house in Levittown, which was the "boonies" then, and decided against it. They probably didn't have enough money. We had no car, no phone, and Levittown didn't have the public transportation we were used to. I'm glad they decided to remain in Richmond Hill!

Chapter 3

I always thought that we all attended St. Benedict Joseph Labre School from kindergarten through eighth grade. I found out that George, Dolores, Reenie, and Jeri went to kindergarten and first and second grades at PS 53, located on 114th Street, just south of Atlantic Avenue. (Little did we know we would end up living on that street one day.) My brother and sisters were eventually switched over to St. Bennies when there was room. I started kindergarten at St. Bennies at age 4 ½. I was kind of skinny, so they probably squeezed me in! Kindergarten was nothing like it is today. We sang songs, had play time, and a story was read to us by Sister Simplicia. We played in a little wooden house with a table and chairs and a play set of dishes, took a nap on a blanket on the floor, once in a while had a snack of milk, and went home. It was half a day kindergarten, and Mom usually picked me up with my younger sisters in tow.

There was no tuition at St. Bennies when I went. Our pastor, Monsignor Hald, was the Superintendent of Schools for the Brooklyn Diocese, and I later discovered that we had the best teachers at St. Bennies due to Msgr. Hald's position. We were taught by the Sisters of St. Joseph. They wore habits that consisted of an ankle-length, long-sleeved, heavy black dress with rosary beads hanging from the waist, a long black veil, and heavily starched, white material that covered the forehead, sides of the face, and hung down into a bib, which covered their neck and chest. As kids we used to wonder if they had hair and normal body parts. And it seemed they never went to the bathroom! I'm sure all that starch was sometimes responsible for the occasional short temperedness, especially in the hot weather.

I was *never* good in math. The first grade teacher, Miss Glenn, the only lay teacher in the school, was obviously older because she didn't wear a habit and her grey hair showed. Even though her face wasn't surrounded by starch, she was strict and mean. One day during math she used her "pointer" stick to point at numbers on the blackboard and asked me what the total was. As I was nervously trying to come up with the answer, she hit me on top of my head with the pointer stick. I was petrified, she was very mad, and to this day I believe it is the reason I don't like math. Anyway, it's a good excuse. I fit right in with today's "blame somebody else" crowd.

An experience I will never forget in Miss Glenn's first grade class was the day she asked whose parents were not Catholic. I obediently raised my hand and told her my mother was Protestant. Miss Glenn was quick to inform me that my mother was going to hell because she was not Catholic. I felt like crying. Hell had already been fully described as this ever-burning place where bad people went and suffered for eternity. I was only 5 years old, totally innocent and unaware of different religions, and it scared me.

I went home for lunch, sat on the couch, and told Mom I didn't want lunch because Miss Glenn said she was going to hell because she wasn't Catholic. Mom said nothing, except to tell me to go in and eat my lunch, which I did. I was never told what happened, but I know that when Dad came home from work, Mom had on a suit and a hat, and they went to Miss Glenn's house. When they came home, not a word was said. In today's world, the parents would come home and tell the kids, "I told that old #+$*#?& off," and disrespect for authority would be encouraged. I am so thankful Mom and Dad didn't cower and accept the religious bias that was taught and had the guts to stand up against it. As the years passed, I came to realize that when Mom put on her suit and hat, *big business* was at hand!

When Dolores was old enough to join Girl Scouts, it seems there wasn't enough room for her in the troop at St. Bennies. Mom then enrolled her in the Girl Scout Troop at a nearby Lutheran Church and—*lo and behold*—there was suddenly room available for Dolores at St. Bennies! Thank God for Mom and her gumption to deal with such blatant unfairness. I, for one, was often aware of the unspoken prejudice of having a mother who was not Catholic.

While living on 117th Street, we were blessed again with a new baby. Much to my father's and brother George's delight, I'm sure, Raymond was born on January 16, 1949, my 7th birthday! He was another beautiful ten-pound, blonde, green-eyed baby to love. But he, like all of us, wasn't going to be the center of attention for too long. On May 27, 1950, my brother Edward was born. He was a blonde, blue-eyed bundle of joy. His eyes from day one were a really light, sparkling blue like Grandpa Wolf's. Now Raymond had a new playmate, and we had a new baby brother to take care of. Mom told us that Eddie was born a "blue baby." She went to the hospital in labor. The doctor said she wasn't ready, but Mom insisted it was time. Another doctor familiar with my mother and her seven previous births delivered ten-pound Eddie with no complications or negative results.

In second grade, because I was tall, I sat in the last seat of the row next to a boy. One day he said, "Psst—wanna see something?" I looked down, and it was no big deal. My baby brother had one of them. I knew what he did was wrong and went home and told Mom what happened. She quietly listened and said it was good I told her. I don't remember seeing her suit and hat, but I do know the boy next to me wasn't in school anymore. For three weeks straight, when the nun came around marking papers, she gave me an A every time and told me I was a good girl for telling my mother. I didn't realize, being so young, how blessed I was to have parents who dealt with this stuff, even though we lived in a "hush-hush" society.

Of course, as kids the nuns who taught us seemed like old ladies. In reality, most of them were young women dedicated to teaching and doing God's work. One thing was for sure—there was no messing around! We went to school from nine to twelve, walked home real fast, ate lunch, and ran back to school for the one to three afternoon classes. We started each day with a prayer and the Pledge of Allegiance. We had one teacher for the full day and only switched rooms for music, which was taught by Sister Marie DeMontfort, who introduced us to quite an array of songs.

We did not wear school uniforms at St. Bennies, and the Upton kids wore the same outfit for three days and another outfit for the next two. We didn't have a lot of money, but we all dressed nicely. The girls wore dresses; the boys wore shirts and ties. Some of the clothes were hand-me-downs from neighbors or relatives. Mom had a black lamb's wool coat, probably from before she got married, that I wore to school in the winter. I felt grown up and pretty in it, never suspecting that my parents didn't have the money to get me a child's coat. One thing I learned from day one of school is that you obey the nuns and do everything you're told. In my class—in one room—we had sixty-three students; you could hear a pin drop. And the nuns had clickers. We sat, stood, knelt, turned, walked, and stopped at the sound of a clicker. From the start of day, after the Pledge of Allegiance and a prayer, we learned! We had Spelling, Arithmetic, Penmanship, English, History, and Geography. On Friday afternoon we had art. We did finger painting and a lot of wonderful, fun things. The artwork was then displayed in the classrooms and halls for all to see.

All the subjects were taught with enthusiasm. I loved the English lessons and the way we were taught to be descriptive and use adjectives. Grassy hills weren't just that; they were rolling knolls wrapped in lush green velvet. We were taught tricks for how to remember the spelling of words that could be difficult or confused with a sound-alike word. When doing "desert" and "dessert", one student, Joey, got up and said, "Dessert is sloppy slurp," and it has stuck with me through the years. History and Geography were exciting to me because of the detailed way they were taught. I could picture in my mind the places and events being talked about. Unfortunately, I always did lousy in math.

After we learned to print the alphabet, we were taught handwriting. We would do a letter at a time and fill each line of a full page with one letter until we got it right. Practice, practice, practice! Then we were allowed to use pens. The pens were thin wood, and the pen point was a small, slender metal device that we dunked into ink wells in an opening in the corner of our desks. A boy in my class (I'm not squealing) got in a lot of trouble for dunking a girl's long braid into his inkwell.

We made our First Communion when we were 7, and it was always a holy and festive occasion. George wore a suit with knickers and looked so handsome, from the pictures I've seen. Dolores, me, Reenie, Jeri, and Lorraine each wore a beautiful white dress and veil, not necessarily new, and had a white purse that contained rosary beads and our first missal. The nuns made sure the First Communion went perfect. We were directed to walk, kneel, stand or sit with the sound of their clickers, and everyone paid strict attention. We looked like little angels. Dressed for the special occasion, Mom and Dad were always there, with the baby and the rest of the kids, taking pictures with their Brownie camera. The first communicant had pictures taken on the altar and by various statues, and of course with Mom and Dad and the bouquet of flowers they bought. I had a lot of my communion pictures taken while holding baby Raymond, who was 4 months old then.

After First Communion we all walked as a family, baby carriage and all, from our house on 117th Street to our Aunt Marion's house on 92nd Street in Woodhaven. Going to Aunt Marion's on a sacramental day was like getting approval from "the head Catholic" in the family. She was my father's oldest sister who raised her brothers and sisters when my grandparents died, which I understand was kind of an Irish traditional responsibility. She also took care of her Aunt Anna Boyle and Uncle Tom Boyle (Grandma Upton's brother and sister), who both lived with her. Old Uncle Tom was an alcoholic. When he went on a binge, Aunt Marion would go find him and bring him home. She never married, because she was too busy taking care of the needs of others. She was a saintly Christian in our midst. She was the only aunt in the Upton family who sent us all birthday cards every year.

Aunt Marion worked for a book-distributing company and had a nice house with fine furniture, and it was a comfortable place to visit. Between her hall and living room there were pocket doors, which slid into the walls when opened. We used to quietly play "train" and open and close the doors at the next "station." The only passengers getting on and off the trains were my brother and sisters and cousins, Ann and Howie. Aunt Marion usually treated all of us to a piece of her home-made carrot cake. Delicious! We behaved, didn't damage anything, and had fun! In those days, we were raised to live the phrase, "Children are to be seen, not heard."

Before we received First Communion, we had to first receive the sacrament of penance and go to confession and tell the priest our sins. That was a nerve-wracking experience loaded with guilt! Saturday confessions were a weekly event in our house. Mom constantly reminded us, as well as the nuns. To be honest, it became kind of rote. "I disobeyed my parents 136 times, I smacked someone, I stuck out my tongue, I teased my sister, and I chewed gum." We were told we had to wear a hat to church at all times. If we forgot it, we would go as far as hair pinning a tissue on our heads so God wouldn't strike us dead! (In today's church, you're lucky if all body parts are covered!) Sometimes we would stop in the church, which was always open for a visit, light a devotional candle, and kneel and say some prayers at the altar in a nice, peaceful atmosphere. Unfortunately, today's society does not allow the opportunity to do that, and most churches are kept locked. There are no more real candles to light any more, either; you now push a button to turn on the candle. So today, in the name of safety and progress, we now have "push-button prayer"!

Mom made sure we obeyed all the rules of the Catholic church and was 100% supportive of anything we were involved in. One time I had the honor of bringing home the statue of Our Lady of Fatima from school overnight. The base of the statue unscrewed, and inside was a set of rosary beads from Fatima, the city where a miracle occurred. It was a very special privilege to have this statue in our home, and we all—Mom, Dad, and all the kids—knelt on the living room floor and prayed the rosary.

In the Upton household, education came first, no questions asked. Mom made it a top priority, and homework and school grades were number one. If by chance one of us got in trouble in school, we were also punished at home, no excuses or alibis accepted. The passing grade when we went to school was 75, but we would have been grounded for life if we came anywhere near that. I had a pretty tough act to follow. George was always smart and was skipped a grade to keep him occupied in class. Dolores was pretty, smart and a high 90s student. Then there was me – arms, legs, and mouth - tall, skinny, and an 89 average student. Mom was strict about schoolwork; if you got a 98, *why didn't you get 100?* I was always a good speller, loved geography and history, but math was not my thing.

While living on 117th Street, there were only eight children. (*Ha!*) We all had chores to do and were always busy. For fun, we played outside, and the rule was that we *always* watched out for our brothers and sisters. We played tag, Ring-a-lievio, hopscotch, I Declare War, jump rope, stoop ball, and of course, stickball. If a car was coming down the street, the warning call was "car, car—c-a-r," and everybody ran to the side. We had a lot of other kids to play with. A family up the street had seven kids, and Whitey, an only child, was always out there with us. Mom encouraged us to go out to play and get our exercise. My sisters and I were tomboys, and I for one have no regrets. I'm pretty sure that our playing outside also gave Mom a little quiet time with her precious babies.

We used to rollerskate on the sidewalk or in the street. The metal, expandable skates we used had clamps that held them onto the front of our shoe and leather straps that buckled around our ankles. They were useless if you didn't have a skate key to tighten the clamps. We skated on the sidewalk at first, skimming our knees plenty of times, wiping them off, and continuing to skate. When we skated in the streets we had to be real cautious about cars. Sometimes, due to inexperience, it was hard to stop, so we just grabbed onto the nearest tree, parked car, or person to slow down. We eventually had to relinquish our skates to the next sister waiting in line. Usually it was a welcome relief, because by then it was time to put a cold rag on the ankles, which were sore and irritated from the leather straps. But we loved roller skating!

For Halloween we all got dressed in home-made costumes and went door to door for trick-or-treat. Candies, cookies, jelly apples, nickels and dimes, and all sorts of goodies were our treats. Always staying together, we pirates, baseball players, hobos, ghosts, cowboys, princesses, and monsters had to be careful that the paper treat bags didn't get a hole in them, or we'd lose our goodies! On Thanksgiving Day we did the *then*-traditional custom of going "begging." We'd dress as hobos in rag clothes. Singeing an old piece of cork, our faces were smudged and covered with black, sooty ashes, enhancing our vagabond appearance as we went to our neighbors to "beg." We received a variety of apples, pears, and oranges with a penny, nickel, or dime squished inside of them. That came to an end when St. Bennies announced it was not proper to go "begging" on Thanksgiving. Instead, we all stayed home and feasted on the big, scrumptious turkey Mom made and always argued over who was getting the crispy turkey tail!

During the winter, we all went out in the snow to play. Somehow there were always enough hats, gloves, and boots. And if there weren't, we went out anyway! Sometimes to prepare we would put our hats and gloves on the radiators, which were sizzling hot. When we came in from the snow, shaking from the cold, we dried our clothes—jackets, pants, hats, gloves—on the radiators so they'd be dry for our next venture out! Radiators were also good for warming up pajamas at bedtime.

Radiators were great, but in order to keep them warm we had to go down the cellar—spooky!—to make sure there was coal in the furnace. There were two coal bins, one for us and one for the downstairs tenants. Now and then the coal man would come to make a delivery, open the basement window, and scuttle the coal down into the bin. We used a shovel to put the coal into the furnace, and a roaring blaze would appear. The ashes would be scooped out and put into a metal can to cool off before being disposed of. I don't know if the heat was included in the rent or if my parents paid for the coal deliveries, but I do know that some nights it was cold—*brrrr!* Mom and Dad often covered us with coats to keep us warm in bed. I guess we didn't have enough money to buy more blankets.

Our after-school hours were spent doing homework, and even though Mom was busy, she always seemed to find the time to help us when needed. She used to patiently help me with arithmetic, but it took me a long time to get the message. Sorry, Mom. George and Dolores, both very smart, were also helpful with homework. As we got older, we all pitched in and helped our younger siblings with any problems. *Only* after our homework was done, we could go out and play or sometimes run an errand before dinner. Then Daddy would come home from work, and we'd all eat our supper, help feed the little ones, and get them ready for bed. Then we'd wash and dry the dishes, sweep the kitchen floor, and settle down in the living room. We would color, play with our dolls, or play a game of checkers or Parcheesi. George's favorite game was "Peck's Bad Boy." Many times my parents would turn on the Victrola, put on some records, and enjoy listening to their music. They were always romantic and affectionate and would just get up and dance with each other. Les Paul and Mary Ford were favorites, as were the Ink Spots and Mills Brothers. "Auf Wiedersehen" was often played, as was Guy Lombardo and his band of renown. Mom liked Matt Munro and Johnny Ray, and "You'll Never Know" by Rosemary Clooney was a favorite of hers.

Many nights we all listened to the radio. If there wasn't room on the couch, there was on the floor, as we huddled around this three or four foot high piece of furniture and listened to *Amos & Andy, The Lone Ranger, The Shadow, Gangbusters, Ozzie & Harriet,* and a lot of mystery shows that my father especially liked. We were all engrossed listening to Walter Winchell as his stirring voice broadcasted national and worldwide news. Imaginations were stirred as we envisioned the stories that were being aired.

Chapter 4

In 1950, the Korean War broke out. We all learned about air-raid sirens and that if we heard them it meant we were being attacked and had to go to a safe place. There were dark shades covering our windows so the "enemy" wouldn't see lights and a lot of talk about air raid shelters. We had air raid drills in school, which were pretty frightening. If the air raid sirens went off, we were supposed to get under our desks so we wouldn't get hurt when bombs fell. The newsreels in the movies showed our soldiers plodding in rag-covered boots through icy snow in Korea. For years after the war ended, the air raid sirens rang every Friday at noon to make sure they were working. It was a grim reminder.

I had a friend named Roseanne who lived across the street. She had a fenced-in yard, and we played dress up and wore some old clothes to play house or pretend we were on stage. One time I was strutting and singing "The Daughter of Rosie O'Grady" at the top of my lungs. (I saw the movie with Mom.) Her Italian family was probably cringing at the sound of this Irish song. But I was lucky because Roseanne's family was the first to get a television. As her friend, I went there to watch this newfangled, magical thing and had to be home at 7:30. Roseanne only lived across the street and about 5 houses down, but Mom gave me strict instructions on how to be careful. Don't walk on the sidewalk; there could be someone hiding in the bushes! Don't walk near the cars; someone could grab you and take you away! Walk in the middle of the street, look up in the trees, stay away from everything—and walk fast! I kid around to this day that I'm lucky I don't have neck problems, but I am very thankful for the awareness that was instilled at a very young age and remains with me to this day.

We eventually got our own television and all sat around watching this small-screened treasure. We all *loved* Lucy! We were introduced to the Our Gang Rascals, the Three Stooges, Laurel and Hardy, Abbott and Costello, Gene Autry, Roy Rogers, Flash Gordon, Red Skelton, Ed Sullivan, and more. Mom didn't like Milton Berle, so we didn't watch him. TV could only be watched after supper, and *only* if our homework and chores were done—no ifs, ands, or buts! Education came first!

We lived on 117th Street until I was 9 years old. It was a different world compared to today. We had street vendors who used push carts to sell their wares. The man who sharpened knives, scissors, etc., would come around ringing his bell, and anyone needing his services would have it done before their eyes. The vegetable man also pushed his cart for all to see the variety of fresh vegetables and fruit to choose from. If the price was right, or Mom haggled over the cost, we sometimes purchased from the street vendor. Mom always reminded the vendor how many children she had, and he would drop the price to sell a large amount of his produce. Mom was good and carefully watched every hard-earned penny, nickel, and dime.

We even had a man with a pony cart come around, offering rides for 10¢ a person. The cart was on two big wheels, and the driver sat in the front to direct the pony. On *very rare* occasions we climbed in the opening in the back of the uncovered cart, sat on the cushioned seats on each side, and proceeded to take our "world tour"—around the block! For 10¢, we rode past our neighbors and friends and felt like a million! This usually occurred when Grandpa Wolf or Uncle Bumpsy treated us.

Grandma and Grandpa Wolf were a big part of our lives, and

we saw them frequently. I often wondered if they were concerned that Mom had been so sick and continued having babies. They bought a small candy store in Richmond Hill on Jerome Avenue and 111th Street. They sold ice cream, candy, fresh-made sodas, and egg creams to delight the sweet toothed. Outside was a wooden, bench-like table where all the daily newspapers were on display. A convenient barber shop for Dad and George was two doors down, obvious by its swirled, striped pole. Quite often we walked as a family to visit Grandma and Grandpa at their store.

Grandma and Grandpa Wolf eventually bought a larger candy store on Rockaway Boulevard and 115th Street in Ozone Park. Wolf's popular candy store offered fresh coffee, hot chocolates, ice cream sodas, frappes (sundaes), and *real* malteds. Since it was right down the street from Our Lady of Perpetual Help church, Sundays were overflowing with customers buying newspapers and goodies. Neighborhood kids carefully chose their penny candies from behind the glass-enclosed case, which was constantly wiped down and kept clean. The 2¢ long, skinny pretzels sold like hotcakes. Many Sundays I would walk with a sister or a friend (had no trouble getting someone willing to go to Wolf's candy store), and we'd help with the penny-candy sales while Grandma and Grandpa were busy serving behind the stool-seated counter.

Sometimes if they were running out of coins, Grandpa would offer to go next door to the deli to get change. Grandma usually went instead, because she was shrewd and on to his mischievous ways, knowing he would go two doors further down to the bar and grill, get the change—and have a quick schnapps! She ran a tight ship and wasn't going to let him go overboard! Grandma made sure everything was kept clean and spotless in the store as she did in her own home. All the cups, glasses, and silverware were washed and dried by hand, which we helped with when there. Before leaving to go home, we swept the floors and the walkway in front of the store. Then a frappe was made for us and we'd sit in the back room reading the latest comic books while eating it. With a hug and a kiss, we were given the nickel or dime for the bus ride home.

Back then, a lot of chores were done by hand. Appliances were quite different from today's modern household conveniences. In our kitchen, we had an "ice box" to refrigerate our food. The ice man would deliver a huge piece of ice. He used big tongs with claws that gripped the ice, put it on his shoulder and back, and carried it up the stairs. The ice was placed in the top insulated compartment of the ice box, and the ice kept everything cold until it melted. Then Mom would clean the ice box and order more ice. Sure enough—the ice man cometh! We also had our bottles of Renken milk delivered. A lot of kids—a lot of milk! I'm sure Mom worked out a special price for the quantity needed. If all the milk didn't fit in the ice box, in the winter Mom put it outside on the window ledge, along with the butter, to keep it cold. When there was a milk strike we had to walk to Borden's on 126th Street and Atlantic, wait in a long line, and buy whatever milk we were allowed to be rationed.

In those days, there were no toasters as we know today. It's hard to describe, but picture a thin metal disc with a hole in the center. Attached to the outside of the disc were four bread-sized pieces of metal wires that extended to the middle of the "toaster." The metal disc was placed on the stovetop, bread was laid on the metal wires, and the gas flame was turned on. The bread would toast on one side and be turned over to toast the other side, and then we'd get the butter and jelly and enjoy our toast, being careful not to burn our fingers. *Ouch!*

Wherever we went we always walked, since we didn't have a car. We walked to Liberty Avenue to shop. There was an A&P and many open market fruit and vegetable stands. Mom carefully looked over each and every potato, string bean, carrot, banana, apple, or anything she was buying. Then she *always* checked to see that the scale was correct. If it wasn't, she didn't buy, because she wasn't going to be gypped! There was a dairy store just off Lefferts Boulevard where we bought pullet eggs at the lowest price. They also sold cracked eggs, which we bought for even less money and used for scrambled eggs, French toast, or cake mixes. Whatever! Mom loved limburger and Swiss cheese and bought them if the price was right and the Swiss cheese had enough holes in it! A huge piece of Romano Italian cheese was gotten and shredded at home to blanket our spaghetti dinners. Delicious!

Then the highlight: Carvers Jewish Bakery on Liberty Avenue, just off Lefferts Boulevard. Mom and Dad each had a sweet tooth, and we always had cake, jelly donuts, or crumb buns after supper, even though money was tight. One of us older ones would stay outside to watch the baby, or babies, who were in the carriage while Mom made the selection. Just looking in the window of Carvers Bakery was a treat; you just wanted a taste of everything! Dad very often brought home huge, scrumptious layer cakes, made by the Greek bakers in Astoria, near where he worked.

If Mom sent us to the "avenue" to buy something, it was always with definite instructions. The jelly donuts had to be the "largest and most sugar covered." The dozen crumb buns had to have "the most crumbs, and no ends"—just crumby center pieces. I would easily recite the order of "a small Jewish rye bread with seeds, sliced thin." I'd carefully watch the loaf of rye go through the slicer, making sure the end wasn't discarded. Mom told me to watch to make sure I wasn't getting cheated. By the way, even though we bought these goodies, don't think we got the whole thing. The jelly donuts and crumb buns were cut in half or less, and the seven-tiered layer cakes with chocolate icing were sliced real thin, as if cut with a razor.

It was the same thing at Trunz meat store, where we got our cold cuts. As Mom instructed, we ordered frankfurters, specifying explicitly that there be at least "ten or twelve to a pound." The bologna was to be sliced thin enough so you "could read a newspaper through it." And if it wasn't right, back to the store we went! If we were shortchanged a penny or two, we had to go back and fight for what was due. I never liked being sent to the avenue by myself. I used to try to talk my sisters into going with me, and even tried bribery! I'd say, "I'll pay you a nickel" or "I'll buy you a long, skinny pretzel" (which was 2¢), but they rarely fell for it. Many times I was told to take my brothers, which of course included the baby in the carriage. The carriage was needed to put the groceries in anyway.

The baby carriage was a very deep-bodied one. On one trip, Eddie, who was 1 one year old, was the youngest, and was strapped in. Raymond, who was 2, was put in backward, facing Eddie. Sometimes I'd run with the carriage just to make them laugh. I loved looking at their happy, dimpled faces and smiling eyes. It usually worked out fine, except when I had to buy a 50 pound bag of potatoes. Then it became a little precarious as they were perched on top of the potatoes—especially when I had to tilt the carriage to cross the street. But we all made it home safe—Ray, Eddie, and the potatoes! These shopping ventures continued on with the babies who were born after them. Those big, deep-bodied carriages were great for holding everything!

When we went shopping for clothes and shoes, we usually went into Jamaica, many times to Goodwins. Quite often Mom took us by train to Kleins on 14th Street at Union Square. Whatever was bought was always on sale. Mom believed in buying a coat, dress, shoes—whatever—in a larger size so we had room to grow into it. Everything, of course, was passed down to the younger ones. Very little was thrown out. We learned to sew buttons back on, baste or back stitch a torn seam or hem, and sewed patches on holes in our pants and dungarees. If new shoes were purchased, taps were put on the heels to preserve their wear. All shoes in need of repair were taken to the shoemaker for new soles and heels. If we didn't have the money to have shoes repaired and the soles were worn thin or had a hole in them, we put a piece of cardboard inside to extend its use. It worked great! If a shoelace broke, tie a knot in it and keep using it! If shoes or sneakers were worn enough to throw in the garbage, the laces were first removed and kept for future use. Nothing was wasted, and Mom made sure we got our money's worth out of everything. *Nothing* was handed to us! If we wanted something, we had to earn the money to buy it. As we got older, newspaper routes, babysitting, house cleaning, sweeping a neighbor's walkway, running errands, or stocking shelves for a nearby business is how we did it. If you worked for it and saved your money until you had enough, you could buy it! To this day, whatever I buy is on sale, on clearance, or with a coupon! It's in my blood!

We were always made aware of the value of a penny, nickel, or dime, and constantly reminded not to waste anything, especially when it came to the utilities. "Close that door—you're wasting the heat!" "If you're chilly, put on a sweater." "Shut those lights off! Do you think our name is Edison?" "Close that door. Do you think you live in a barn?" "Shut that window. We're not paying to heat the neighborhood!" "Stop running the water. It costs money." When washing the dishes, we filled a big pot with hot, soapy water and were told to wash them—*then* turn the water on to rinse them all at once. Don't waste water running down the drain for nothing! "Don't fill the tub to the brim with hot water. Where do you think you live, the Taj Mahal?" "Put the lights out if no one's in the room!" "Close that refrigerator door—it costs money to run!" Believe me, we all learned the value of saving money to keep costs down. To this day, I will fight for a penny or a nickel; ask the local supermarket managers!

At no cost whatsoever, Mom took us to the neighborhood parks all the time. We walked to the park on 125th Street. It was nicknamed "Smokey Park" because it was right across the street from the Long Island Railroad train yard on Atlantic Avenue, and in those days the trains were fueled with coal. The smoke from the trains was consistent, and the soot would travel in the air and lightly settle in the park on the benches, swings, sliding ponds, monkey bars, etc. There was also a pool at Smokey Park, but nothing like the swimming pools today. It was a large, cement-floored pool with a black wrought-iron fence surrounding it and a drain in the center. Around the sides of the pool, set in cement, were sprayers of water, which were very cool and refreshing to run through. We usually went home feeling refreshed but with sore feet from scraping them on the cement floor.

There was also a park on Liberty Avenue and 102nd Street, right next to the police station, which we walked to quite often. The usual swings, monkey bars, and slides were ours to enjoy. The park on 106th Street and Atlantic Avenue had no pool but instead had a large, upright sprinkler, which was invigorating to run through or sit under to cool off. Then there was Forest Park, where we walked to on many a Sunday afternoon. That was a hike! With their arms around each other or holding hands, Mom and Dad always enjoyed the free concerts that were held there, and we were all treated to a ride on the carousel. Dressed in our Sunday outfits, we older kids took special care of the younger ones so they wouldn't get hurt. Needless to say, we were all tired from the long walk and had no trouble falling asleep once we got back home.

When we lived on 117th Street, my sisters and I played with our dolls. We played house and took care of our babies. We "made believe" fed them, changed their diapers, bathed them, and gently wrapped them nice and warm so they could sleep. Dolls in those days were rubber baby dolls. They weren't developed, didn't have boyfriends, and had no detailed body parts! On a nice day, we would take our dolls for a walk in the stroller or in the carriage with whoever was the baby at the time. We also played quietly with cut-out paper dolls that came on a sheet of paper with a variety of paper outfits. We would dress our paper dolls by bending the tags on their outfits over their shoulders, arms, and waists. Wearing paper dresses, coats, bathing suits, shoes, and all sorts of outfits, our paper dolls would converse and interact with each other, and we *all* had a good time in our make-believe world.

My younger brothers were always busy playing with their toys. Wooden clothespins at the time were very inventive items and were used to build an imaginary house or fort. For the baby, the clothespins were put in a container, and the challenge was to get the lid off. Confrontations also took place between their miniature plastic cowboys, Indians, and soldiers. Playing cowboys and shooting fake guns was part of being a boy then. One of the best and most fun things was a big refrigerator-size cardboard box. The end flaps were usually the entry to our "house" with cut out "windows," or a fort used for protection against the attacking enemy. It didn't cost a dime but put young minds to good use. There was *always* a baby swing hanging in the doorway of the living room. I can still hear my brothers laughing and giggling with delight as they swung back and forth.

George and Dolores were each in scouts and were involved

in all sorts of troop activities. We'd all watch George fill his backpack for a Boy Scout camping trip and stuff it with his flashlight, metal canteen, metal plates and eating utensils, and a variety of knives for the adventure. When finished, I think the backpack weighed more than him. The troop would sleep and cook outdoors, and when he returned after the weekend away, he looked pretty beat. But George loved it! Dolores was involved in everything her troop did, especially selling Girl Scout cookies. Dad took her in uniform to West Chemical where he worked, and naturally she was the top cookie seller in the troop. The rest of us girls also joined Girl Scouts. Forest Park was where we went for a cook-out and learned how to start our own fire and disperse the ashes safely. The hot dogs and marshmallows were good, but that outdoorsy stuff wasn't my bag.

Of course in those early days—the 1940s and early '50s—we just enjoyed our playthings and didn't know where they came from. There was a very nice man, Mr. Dunn, who would stop by around Christmastime. He represented the St. Vincent de Paul Society at St. Bennies, the organization that helped the poor and needy in the parish. On Christmas morning we would awaken to a variety of new or used gifts—dolls, doll clothing, a wagon, a scooter, games, used or new clothes, new underwear and socks for all of us, dungarees, toys for all of us, a cowboy hat and gun, a bicycle. If it was a used bicycle, Dad brought the handlebars into work to have them re-plated and made shiny like new. Used or not, Santa had definitely been to our house! It was so different from today's world, where requests are made for expensive clothes, computers, cars, etc. We were never asked what we wanted for Christmas and totally appreciated whatever we received.

Speaking of Christmas on 117th Street, there was an old Scandinavian couple—the Ks—who lived diagonally across the street from us and always had a very big Christmas tree that was highly decorated. They spoke with an accent, and Mr. K smoked a pipe. Much to our delight, my sisters and I were invited over to see the tree. While looking at the tree, Mr. K said, "Patty, come in the kitchen; I have some ice cream for you to take home for your brothers and sisters." I followed Mr. K through the swinging kitchen door. Suddenly he grabbed me, was holding me tight, and was trying to kiss me. He had big, flabby, blubbery, fat lips that stunk from pipe smoking. I was 7 years old, petrified, and had been taught to *never* be disrespectful to an adult. Thank goodness my sister Reenie opened the swinging door a little and said, "Patty, what's taking you so long?" We went right home, with no ice cream, and Mom was at the kitchen sink preparing vegetables. I very anxiously and secretively told her what happened, and she calmly said I was right to tell her. Things like that were hushed in those days. When Daddy came home from work, Mom was dressed in her suit and hat, and they went over to the Ks' house. Upon their return, we were told never to go over to the Ks' house again. There was no explanation, no police, end of subject. Again, Mom's suit and hat meant *serious business was at hand.*

Unbeknownst to us kids, we were poor and didn't have much money. There were eight of us, and I'm sure things were tight financially. Before Ray and Eddie were born, in 1948 my father started going to the *New York Times* to try and make some extra money. Dad would put in a full day's work at West Chemical and then go to 42nd Street and Times Square to "shape." A lot of men were there looking for work, and it depended on if you were chosen or not whether you earned a night's pay. We didn't have a phone, so if Dad didn't come home, it meant he was picked. He then went to his factory job the next morning. Sometimes he would get off early enough to come home for a few hours of sleep. Many a night Dad would come home at midnight or 1:00 AM, tired and frustrated because he didn't get on. But it didn't stop him. He attempted to work every night and Saturdays to earn extra money for our ever-growing family, and his undying diligence and years of shaping finally paid off. He earned his Union Card at the *New York Times* in 1954. *A second permanent, full-time job!*

To this day we don't know how Daddy did it. He worked at West Chemical from 7:00 AM to 4:00 PM from Monday to Friday. Then on Tuesday, Wednesday, Thursday, and Friday nights, he worked at the *New York Times* as a mailer. He worked a full day on Saturdays and Saturday night too. When he had the chance he would sleep between shifts on stacks of newspaper. He even took what little time he had to buy Mom flowers or her favorite fruit-slices candy. But no matter how long he worked, how many hours he put in, how exhausted he was, when Dad got off work early Sunday morning, he *always* went to the early "Printer's Mass" at Holy Cross Church on 42nd Street. The power of love and faith is incredible. What an example of sacrifice, dedication, and hard work he set for all of us to follow.

Of course, these times were a strain on Mom, who was home running the ship by herself many times. But thank God, we couldn't have asked for a better Captain! I know Mom missed Daddy very much. To keep us in line, maintain discipline, and make sure we listened, Mom always had a leather strap, one of Daddy's belts, around her neck. When we were told to do something, the threat of the strap was there—and suddenly our hearing improved dramatically! Mom watched every penny like it was a piece of gold. Grandma Wolf used to say Mom held a nickel so tight she made the buffalo move! I was once sent on my bike to the Richmond Hill Savings Bank on Liberty Avenue with the savings account passbook and a nickel to deposit. When I got back home and gave her the passbook, Mom looked at it and said, "We're five cents better off than we were last week." That sense of saving was instilled in all of us, and eventually we each had our own savings account. Not long ago I was in a small deli when this boy about 14 ran in, was in a rush, grabbed a candy bar, and threw his money on the counter. In his haste, he dropped a coin on the floor. I told him and he quickly looked down and said, "Eh—it's only a nickel" and ran out the door. Instantly, the memories of the importance of a nickel came flooding back to me, like when Mom was in the hospital with TB and Dad didn't have the nickel for the bus to visit her. And another time …

When Lorraine was 3 years old, while chasing a ball, she was hit by a car in front of our house on 117th Street. Mom went with Lorraine in the ambulance to Kew Gardens Hospital. Lorraine had a fractured pelvis, a deep gash on her eyebrow, and her jaw was injured and swollen. She was kept at the hospital, but Mom, in her hasty departure, didn't have the five cents for the bus ride home. Spattered with blood, she had to literally beg people for carfare to get home. Finally a woman gave Mom the necessary fare, only after exchanging names and addresses to make sure Mom paid her back, which she did. Every nickel was important then, and still is. It's the pennies, nickels, and dimes that make the dollars.

A few days later, I went with Mom to see Lorraine in the hospital. When we walked in the hospital room, Lorraine was crying, her foot tied to the crib, and the nurse was spanking her! Mom was shocked and pushed the nurse away from her baby. She untied Lorraine, picked up her precious little girl to calm her, and bundled her in a blanket, and we left the hospital and took Lorraine home. Mom was always concerned about Lorraine's fractured pelvis. She feared it would cause future problems and prevent Lorraine from having children. All fears vanished down life's road when Lorraine gave birth to five beautiful, healthy children.

There was nothing too fancy about the way we lived, but everything was super clean. Mom did the wash in a wringer washing machine. She used to stir the clothes around with a stick, and then to get rid of the water, she would run the clothes through the wringer. The wet clothes were put between two bars (the wringer), which were squeezed tight together and cranked with a handle as the clothes went through and the water was squeezed out. They were wrung out and ready to be hung and dried. Then each piece was hung with wooden clothespins on the clothesline outside the kitchen window, which was attached to the pole in the backyard. You had to be real careful not to lean too far out the window. Mom told us that when she was a girl, clothes were cleaned on a washboard. It was a wood-framed gadget, with a ridged metal insert, and the clothes were wet and scrubbed with soap on the metal, by hand.

Our hairdos were simple and easily maintained. Buster Browns for me, Reenie, Jeri, and Lorraine. We all had straight hair, which was cut even to our ears, topped with straight cut bangs. Dolores had a natural wave to her hair, and because she was older, she started curling it. Her hair always looked pretty, so we sisters followed her example. We learned how to make curls with hair pins. One time Mom and Aunt Charlotte (Mom's sister-in-law) gave us perms at home, and we looked like brillo-heads. But we thought we were gorgeous! Down the road, we used wire mesh and foam rubber curlers. George had a "pompadour" and used Brylcreme, which made his black hair look slick. As he got older he used to really fuss and primp and held up the line for the bathroom! We used castile soap to wash our hair and with a comb yanked and pulled the knots out. Who knew about cream rinses or conditioners, which cost extra money? Raymond and Eddie had longer hair for quite a while, but they too ended up with buster browns. Mom always saved the baby hairs from everyone's first haircut and saved any of our baby teeth in individual envelopes.

Even though we didn't have much money, Mom made sure we all went to the dentist. The importance of dental care was always stressed by Mom, who never had a cavity. We drank only milk and weren't allowed to have soda, except on special occasions, because of the damage it caused to teeth. If we had cavities to be filled, we were not allowed to get Novocain as a pain killer because of the extra cost. In those days, the dental drills were grindingly slow and painful and seemed unending. Our dentist, Dr. Shade, was kind enough to give us the numbing medication sometimes and didn't charge Mom for it. What she didn't know didn't hurt us!

Since George was the oldest child, he was left in charge of all of us if Mom and Dad went out. My recollections are of being under the rule of Attila the Hun! He would bully and boss us around, like he was finally able to display his vengeance for having five sisters. I complained to Mom once that he kicked me (actually, I think I kicked him first in self-defense), but nothing was done about it. I guess I was a little feisty, which was not appreciated by my big brother. George got a newspaper route—actually a couple of them—delivering the *Daily News*, the *Long Island Press,* and others. He would get the papers, and we sisters would help triple fold them for tossing. The newspapers were in his bike basket, and as he rode past the houses, he'd toss them on the stoop or lawn. I went to help George in snowstorms, pulling a wagon full of newspapers, sometimes trudging up long walkways to make sure the papers were delivered dry on the stoop or porch. He worked hard to earn some money.

George was a young teen and becoming very aware of clothes and wanted to buy a pair of pegged pants, which were very much in style in the early fifties. The parental answer was *no!* I overheard the discussions when Mom and Dad said there was no way a son of theirs was going to dress like a "hood." It was the same thing with those pointy, hoody shoes (roach squishers) that were part of the '50s scene. The answer was no. End of subject!

Usually if Mom and Dad went out, it was to the Casino movies on Liberty Avenue, the Jerome on 114th Street, the Lefferts movie on Liberty and 124th, or the RKO Keiths on Hillside Avenue and 117th Street. Each show consisted of two full-length movies, a newsreel of world events, a continuing Superman, Buster Crab, or Flash Gordon series, coming attractions, and a cartoon—for the price of 9¢ a person. During the week if Dad was working, Mom took one of us with her to the movies. We saw some great movies, mostly musicals or love stories, and Mom would get all teary eyed about stuff I didn't quite understand. If it was a musical, I loved it and would dance around the house afterward. As kids we spent some Saturday afternoons at the Jerome movie on 114th Street. It was 7¢, and I'm sure Mom and Dad enjoyed some quiet time alone when possible. The really expensive movie to go to was the Valencia in Jamaica. The domed ceilings were covered with clouded blue skies and twinkling stars, for those willing to pay the extra price to impress a date.

Mom knew the neighbors and stopped to talk sometimes but did not have any close friends that I can recall. Her life was concentrated on the family. She was never one to coffee klatch but was always compassionate and caring for those who had less or were lonely and left out. She was *always* a champion of the underdog and tried to make sure that people were treated fairly and taught us to do the same. Up the street was a three-family house, and the N family lived on the third floor, which was actually the attic. They had a cute son, Tommy, who had blue eyes and curly blonde hair, and every day Mr. N would carry him downstairs and put him in a wagon. Tommy had Muscular Dystrophy and couldn't walk. To us, he was just another nice kid to play with. We would pull him in the wagon, have fun, and make him laugh. All we ever saw was this happy, smiling, beautiful boy who enjoyed being with other kids. Then we'd take Tommy back to his house, and his father would carry him upstairs.

Just the other side of Jerome Avenue was Alfred, who was quite a character and came to our house with his mother on a regular basis. (He was about my age.) His mom sometimes left Alfred with us if she had an errand to run. We would read stories, play games, talk, and just plain have fun. Alfred had Cerebral Palsy. He spoke and walked slower, his body would jerk or twitch, but he was a very smart boy who was a lot of fun. When we first met Alfred I asked my mother what was wrong with him. She said nothing was wrong. God made people to be different, but everyone needed friends to make them feel special. Not too many years ago I met Alfred in a supermarket in Richmond Hill, and he remembered the fun he had with the Upton kids. He was with his wife, who also has Cerebral Palsy, and in her wheelchair she was holding their newborn baby, who was absolutely beautiful.

There were a lot of ice cream parlors in Richmond Hill, but the favorite of Mom and Dad's was Hugos, on Liberty and Lefferts. We all walked up there, always pushing a baby carriage, and were greeted warmly by the happy-go-lucky German owner, Hugo. Each of us got a cone, ice cream soda, or frappe (sundae), and Mom always enjoyed her favorite pistachio ice cream soda. George and Dolores were older and sometimes would go with their friends to Ludemann's Ice Cream Parlor on Atlantic and 118th, Karp's on Liberty and Lefferts, or Winters on Liberty and 111th Street. The original Jahn's Ice Cream Parlor on Hillside Avenue and 117th Street was popular with everyone. On your birthday you got a free sundae. Jahn's was famous for its Kitchen Sink, a huge variety of ice creams in an enormous bowl, topped with syrups, marshmallows, sprinkles, nuts, whipped cream, and everything else imaginable. It came with a lot of spoons and was shared with friends. I never had one, but it sure sounded delicious!

There was a Chinese restaurant on Liberty Avenue around 124th Street, above some stores. It was always a special and rare occasion when we went there, walking, of course, with the babies in the carriage. My parents always ordered chow mein with extra rice for all of us to share. (The extra rice made the chow mein stretch further.) Those crispy Chinese noodles that came with it were everyone's favorite. Sometimes we would go on our bikes to pick up chow mein, while Mom cooked extra rice, which was ready when we got home. I never knew until I was older and went with a friend to a Chinese restaurant that they had menus! For years I thought the only thing served in a Chinese restaurant was chow mein! As we got older Mom warned us about Chinese restaurants and "white slavery," which really did exist then. White girls were drugged and shipped off to China, never to be seen again. I was aware and cautious, but a friend of mine says she still can't enjoy Chinese food to this day because of my mom's warnings.

An adventure that was always wonderful was our Sunday outings to Manhattan and a ride on the Staten Island Ferry. We were all dressed in our Sunday best. (Suitable, neat outfits, not fancy or new, and sometimes a little oversized and used). Mom always looked so pretty in a nice dress (*red* was her favorite color), and Dad looked so handsome in his suit. Baby carriage and all, we'd first have to pay to go through the then tall, cage-like, metal turnstiles to get on the trains. We were "such a close family" that my parents squeezed two or three of us through for the price of one. Those nickels were hard to come by! The ferry cost 5¢, and we all enjoyed the ride thoroughly. We'd pass the Statue of Liberty, see some ships and tugboats, and stand by the rail and feel the wind and misty spray on our faces as we watched the ferry plow through the waters. Mom and Dad were always holding hands, had their arms around each other, and were kissing. It was exciting to watch the ferry dock, and everyone was then supposed to leave the boat. Well, since the return trip would have cost another 5¢ for each of us, a few of us kids stayed on board and hid under the benches until the ferry loaded up again. I think the crew was on to us, but no one said a word. As reminded by Mom and Dad, while on deck we all held hands and watched out for each other. On the return trip I was always in awe of the view of the skyscrapers and the enormity of NYC. We would then walk back to the subway station, where a special treat awaited us. A vendor sold pineapple juice for 10¢, and Dad bought us each a cup to share with another sister or brother. All of us enjoyed the Staten Island Ferry and looked forward to the next trip.

Even though we were a growing family (I'll keep you updated) and didn't have money for costly vacations, we did things that other families didn't do. We went every year to Madison Square Garden to see the Rodeo, Barnum and Bailey Circus, and the Ice Capades. The cowboys hung on tight while riding the bucking broncos. It was awesome to watch them on their horses as they lassoed bulls and tied them up with their lariats. We saw Roy Rogers, Dale Evans, and Trigger. At the circus, we saw Marilyn

Monroe riding an elephant while the clowns kept everyone laughing with their funny antics and the trapeze artist swung overhead. Dad usually bought the cheapest tickets (99¢) to all of these events, and we were seated pretty high up and far away from the arena. After the show started, we moved down closer and used seats that were empty. We got the most for the least!

The Ice Capades was a spectacular event to watch as the skaters glided gracefully in their glittering outfits to the sound of an inspiring musical background. We saw the world-famous Norwegian figure skating star Sonja Henie, whose elegant talent was incredible to watch. We even saw Esther Williams at Jones Beach when she swam and starred in the "Aquacades." Sometimes Mom and Dad took us to the boxing matches at Sunnyside Gardens. I was pretty small then and would fall asleep, not really knowing why everyone was yelling and a bell kept ringing. The best part was being carried home in Daddy's arms, sleepy and safe. He was big and strong and somehow managed to carry whoever was too tired to walk, which reminds me of a visit to my father's brother's house.

Uncle Eddie and Aunt Helen Upton lived in Brooklyn, and we took the Myrtle Avenue trolley to Ridgewood, the end of the line. We then walked to their apartment, which was on a street of brick-row houses with steep stairs going to the second floor. Uncle Eddie and Aunt Helen both worked for the telephone company, never had children, and were financially comfortable. They were big into playing the horses and were both heavy drinkers. We children sat quietly while their ugly, yapping chihuahua dog snapped and snarled at us. Once, when Mom and Dad started packing us all up to leave, Uncle Eddie, in his loud, boisterous voice, turned to my father, who was holding two of us, and bellowed, "Boy, George, you're stuck for life carrying kids home."

Dad laughingly responded, "I'd rather carry an armful of kids any time than carry a drunken wife home from the bar." We didn't visit them too often. Thank goodness most of our family ventures were more exciting and fun.

A favorite family trip was going to Radio City Music Hall to see the Rockettes perform—the precision, the long legs kicking in time with the music, the elegant costumes! When there, I was in my own little world and wanted to jump up on stage and join in. At Christmastime, there was always a dazzling holiday display. If we ate out in the city, it was a special treat to go to Horn and Hardharts Automat. At my young age, it seemed almost a magical place. There were enclosed compartments in the walls, each containing a variety of food for selection, which could be seen through a small glass door. My father gave each of us nickels to buy the food we wanted. There were soups, sandwiches, desserts, and more to choose from. I'd put my nickels into the slot by my favorite—macaroni and cheese for 15¢—and the glass door popped open and there was my dinner. It was deeee-licious! The funny thing was, it seemed the more we went there, the more Horn and Hardhart silverware started showing up in our silverware drawer at home! *Hmmmm?* I always wondered if it was the Catholic or the Lutheran!

Chapter 5

Needless to say, since there were eight children already, it was getting a little tight in the apartment on 117th Street. Mom was always the money handler and was socking away those pennies and nickels for roomier living space. It was in November 1951 that Mom and Dad bought a house on 114th Street! We all pitched in and helped do whatever we were told to do in order to move.

There was no moving truck that I recall—probably due to lack of money—and my Uncle Tom Upton (Dad's favorite brother) was there to help since he had a car—an old Ford with a rumble seat. Many trips were made back and forth on moving day with Uncle Tom's car, taking anything that would fit. We filled the baby carriage, stroller, shopping cart, wagons, and bicycle baskets with everything imaginable and walked to our new house. We walked in a caravan and must have looked like a band of gypsies. Uncle Tom and my father had to make a side trip—to the hospital with Mom. On November 29, 1951, our brown-eyed, dark-haired, cute-as-a-button brother Dennis was born. It was truly a *moving* experience! George was 14, Dolores was 13, I was 9, Reenie was 8, Jeri was 6, Lorraine was 5, Raymond was 2 and Eddie was 1. We all walked to our new house on 114th Street between Atlantic and 95th Avenues.

It was a two-family, semi-attached house, and we moved in upstairs. The house attached to us had a bunch of kids upstairs and downstairs, and Bobby and his brother Donald (Red) lived next door on the other side. Across the street were the Keddys and their cousins, Cookie and Andrew, the Smiths, the Nortons, Jimmy, the Tragales, the Melchs—built-in friends for all of us.

We were between Jamaica and Liberty Avenues for shopping and still had access to a variety of trains and buses. Sometime on moving day, Lorraine (the 666 child) was in Uncle Tom's car and saw a spot on the roof of the car. Like a good little 5 year-old, she decided to get rid of the spot. She got some scissors, cut the spot out, and left a gaping hole in the roof. First air-conditioned Ford! Uncle Tom I'm sure was mad, but he didn't hit the roof—it was already damaged!

Our "new" house had a stoop, and the front door opened into the vestibule, which had a door on the left to enter the first-floor apartment. The other door opened to the hall that led back to the basement, and up front was the staircase to our second-floor apartment. We entered the living room, which had a chandelier and a gas-fired fireplace with a mantel and mirror above it. The mantel was filled through the years with baby pictures, prom photos, wedding pictures, bronzed baby shoes, and memories of the Upton family. To the left of the living room were three rooms, all used as bedrooms for Dolores, Reenie, Jerri, Lorraine, and I. A Castro Convertible and some beds were available for us to share, and sometimes we switched beds and sleeping partners. An alcove with a closet was George's turf, and a vinyl folding door was put up to allow him privacy. (I honestly never knew until later on in my teens that there was such a thing as a dining room!) In our house, *everything was a bedroom*.

To the right of the living room was a swinging door that opened to a hall. On the right was a good-sized pantry, which was really handy for storing food, cleaning utensils, paper goods, etc. There was an air shaft with a skylight between the pantry and the bathroom, which was next in the hallway. Eventually a special hose was attached to the tub so we could shower. Opposite these was the kitchen, which was always in use and filled with the aroma of fresh-percolated coffee and had a new electric refrigerator! (No more ice deliveries!) Two bedrooms (*real* bedrooms) were at the end of the hall. One was my parents' room, with a closet, full bedroom set, and the crib where the baby slept. The other room was for the younger boys, who all slept in bunk beds and kept their belongings in the closet and dressers. (When the headlights of the low-flying airplanes from the nearby airports shone into their room, they used to hide and "shoot" the approaching imaginary enemy.) Needless to say, if we were punished and sent to our room, we weren't sure where to go—and it was never empty!

There were dressers that we all shared. We girls had two drawers each to keep our belongings in. We kept track of our own stuff and treated it with care. Dresses and coats were squished in the closet along with George's suit and Boy Scout uniform. Out of necessity, a big metal closet was eventually purchased for storing all the coats. Shoes were on the closet floor, or next to each dresser. Two sweater drawers were stuffed to capacity. Mom bought us nylon scarves for the tops of the dressers, to prevent scratching, and for keeping our mirrors, hair brushes, and combs. We also had a crucifix and room for any pictures we wanted on display. George, now 14, had all his comics and books in his alcove and always complained that he had no privacy. (What was that?) The full basement, where the heating oil tank and furnace (no more coal!) were, was a Godsend for storing things. George set up his Lionel Train set down there, and with great pride always added pieces to it. There was a huge room with shelves for all our games and more. We didn't have a car, but there was a garage where all our bikes, wagons, sleds, snow shovels, baby carriages, baseballs, and bats were kept. All in all, we had more room, and everybody and everything fit in our new house.

Upon moving in, we were all put to work. Dad had us

scraping off wallpaper so he and Uncle Tom could paint. We wet the wall down and used anything that would remove the wallpaper. Tools were scarce, and I used a butter knife. I'm sure Dad's spackle repaired the resulting gouges. In those days, there were no rollers, just a brush and a can of oil-based paint, which required turpentine to be cleaned. Did it stink! Through the years I learned to spackle, sand, paint, use a screwdriver, and hammer in a nail and am thankful for it. Rosie the Riveter, move over and give me some space!

We weren't in the house too long when big water stains appeared on the walls in the two back bedrooms. The walls were literally soaked, leaving heavy stains that came from the rain and snow on the flat roof above. New house, new baby, nine kids—I know my parents scraped together every penny they had to buy the house, which cost $10,000. If they felt like crying from despair, they never displayed their devastation to us. I don't know where they found him or what he charged, but Mr. Castles was the man who went up on the roof with his huge can of tar and repaired the leak. It was winter and snowing. He went into the pantry and up through the skylight to get on the roof to do his work. He came down soaked and cold, and Mom fed him, gave him coffee, and tried drying his wet clothes on the radiator while he did so. He was a big man, kind of gruff, and his hands were rough and worn looking from hard work. He tarred the roof, did an excellent job, and was not needed again. Mom and Dad did what had to be done and overcame another major challenge in their life.

Another heartrending change took place with our move to 114th Street. Our family dog, Lucky, who we all grew to love through the years, had a very hard time adjusting to the move. He kept running back to our old apartment and familiar turf.

Eventually he ran away, was found hiding and sickly in someone's garden, and was taken by the dog catcher. We all missed him, and eventually got a black medium-sized terrier we called Spooky, who was an excellent watch dog. We had kind of another "pet" also. In the kitchen, we had a new clock on the wall. It was a black cat, with a tail that swung back and forth in the opposite direction of the eyes, which moved left and right in unison. As time passed, the eyes broke, and they would move in and out in opposite directions as the tail swung, so we had a cross-eyed black cat clock! We kept it. It fit right in with some of the cockeyed stuff that went on in our house!

The apartment downstairs was rented by a very quiet family of four—kind of fuddy duds. There was a grandmother, a middle-aged couple, and their teenaged daughter. I'm sure to this day they're still getting over the shock of having a couple with nine very active children buy the house and move in overhead. Aspirin sales probably skyrocketed. Eventually they moved out (wonder why?) and a young, friendly couple with two small children moved in. We were the babysitters!

There were so many other kids on the block. It was great! When it snowed, we were all outside building snow forts and having snowball fights. We were told constantly by Mom to take care of each other and stay together when we were outside. "You can argue and fight with each other in the house, but *never* go against your brother or sister outside. Always stick up for each other!" It was drilled into us. We older sisters would take our younger siblings on sleigh rides. I loved watching them slip and slide in the snow and laugh as they scurried to get up. One was cuter than the other! Reenie didn't participate in outdoor activities too much and sometimes stayed indoors. The day would end with all the snowsuits, hats, and gloves being dried on the sizzling hot radiators. Vaseline was used to soothe our rosy red cheeks.

We were always told in no uncertain terms that we had to stick up for each other when the occasion called for it. Lorraine came into the house crying one time, saying the girl across the street hit her. I was told by Mom that I had to go hit this girl back, and I didn't want to. She said if I didn't, I wouldn't get any lunch, and I was hungry. So I went across the street, told the girl never to hit my sister again, smacked her, and went back upstairs for lunch. Another time we were playing stickball in the street and the boy up the street called Lorraine an a-s-s. Well, we weren't allowed to curse, and I hauled off and belted him one. He ran home crying, and a while later the doorbell rang. I opened the front door, and there was his mother—who slapped me across the face. I responded by slapping her back and shut the door. Her husband came over after supper to talk to my dad, and they seemed to just end up talking casually about work. (Mom was adamant about the woman having no right to slap me and would have been mad at Dad if he had gone against his own.) For whatever reason—probably because I was tall—I seemed to be the "chosen" one for the "eye-for-an-eye" events.

Always the lady, Dolores was not feisty or combatant. Reenie was usually pretty quiet and avoided disagreements. Jeri was outgoing and fun, and obviously Lorraine needed defending. One time Lorraine made the poor choice of sitting on the curb where people walked their dogs. I laughed hysterically and took her upstairs to show Mom what she sat in. I was told that since I thought it was so funny I had to clean up the mess. Boy, does Lorraine owe me!

I remember the day—March 5, 1953—when Dad came home from the hospital to announce the arrival of our tenth baby. The girls were on one side of the room, the boys on the other, almost in team competition. Dark-haired, brown-eyed chubby baby Robert was born; the boys won! It really didn't matter—we all won. We all had a new brother to love and take care of. We sisters were sure kept busy with our little brothers. We all knew how to change a diaper, give the baby a bottle, or feed and give them a bath, getting soaked in the process. We risked getting bopped with the tub toys, but what the heck. They were all so cute!

Even though we were not financially rich by any means, we were always taught to share whatever we had with those less fortunate. The example was set, of course, by Mom, the Good Samaritan. There was a man—we never knew his name—who used to go door to door begging for food. I guess you could say he was a bum—a street person—a lost soul. He found food, warmth, and solace when he rang our bell. Mom always fed him hot food, bread, and coffee. As he sat in the kitchen, he would speak of times past when he worked for wealthy people. Although disheveled, unshaven, and wearing shabby clothes, there seemed to be a gentlemanly air of aristocracy in his speech and manner. Mom, who was untrusting of strangers by nature, always listened as he spoke. What she heard was the voice of a man who once had a full, normal existence and who, for whatever reason, had given up on life. Before he left to go back to the streets, Mom rummaged through the closet to find gloves, a scarf, a hat, a sweater, warm socks, an old pair of Dad's shoes, and a few sandwiches for him to take on his journey. One time Mom wasn't home when he came to the door, and we were not allowed to have strangers in during her absence. But we knew what to do because she showed us. We couldn't let him in the apartment, so we set up a table and chair at the bottom of the stairs, cooked up some soup and God knows what else, and sent him on his way with a full belly and a few bologna sandwiches in his pocket. He came back to our house once in a while, and then we never saw him again. Thank you, Mom, for showing us how to share love and comfort with a stranger whose name we did not know, who we knew nothing about, but who was a creature of God—a man in need. We were taught to share what little we had with those who had less.

Chapter 6

Across the street from our house was PS 53, a four-room wooden schoolhouse, which offered free summer programs for the neighborhood kids. We played a variety of indoor games—nok-hockey was a favorite—drew pictures and painted them, played baseball in the schoolyard, and had a variety of competitive events. Miss Culligan, a super-nice lady, was in charge. The summer schedule ended with a day of sports events at PS 108, in Richmond Hill. I always participated in the running races and loved it. Barbara H. worked with Miss Culligan, and she was great. I don't know if it was because she liked us or felt sorry for us, but she and her friend would take us Upton kids for rides in her car to places we never knew about. We went for a picnic to Heckscher State Park which was *way* out on Long Island, and it was quite an adventure. The variety of trees, birds, small animals, and babbling brooks were there for us to see and learn about. That's when Long Island was still the "country." In the name of progress, PS 53 was eventually razed and replaced with garden apartments, leaving us Upton kids with a lot of great memories.

Mom and Dad always believed in keeping us busy so we wouldn't have time to get in trouble. There seemed to be a lot of sports activities for boys, but few, if any, for girls. There was a man in our parish—Karl K.—who tried organizing a girl's basketball team. I guess because of my height and spunk, Mom had him pick me up and take me to participate in a game. I knew absolutely *nothing* about basketball or how to play, and nobody explained it to me. Mr. K. threw the basketball to me and told me to go out on the court and dribble. Well, dribbling to me meant drooling from the mouth, and I wanted no part of it. Looking back, I know I would have been one heck of a good player if it was more organized and someone told me what to do. It wasn't a total failure though—on various occasions I have been referred to as a "basket case", so all was not lost!

During the summer we all went for free swimming lessons at Richmond Hill High School, on 114th Street, just north of Atlantic Avenue. Again, Mom told us to stay together, and take care of each other. Waiting in line to swim became a learning experience for me and my sisters. There was a variety of kids, and some of them were tough and pushy. I guess I inherited some of Mom's feistiness, because *nobody* was going to push my sisters around. With some bantering and standing tall, I never let anyone push us off our place in line. (Of course I had a lump in my stomach hoping the toughies wouldn't hit us.)

I know we were definitely the only kids on the street who went on adventurous trips to the Bronx Zoo, Prospect Park Zoo in Brooklyn, and Central Park Zoo in Manhattan. One of my favorites was exploring the Museum of Natural History. We would spend hours with Mom and Dad learning about and seeing wonderful exhibits of a world that no longer existed. The prehistoric displays of humongous and frightening dinosaurs kept us staring in awe, thankful they didn't exist anymore. Sometimes we would walk as a family to the firehouse on 121st Street off Atlantic Avenue. Always greeted with smiles by the friendly firemen, they delighted in showing us the equipment they used, let us slide down the fire pole, and of course let all of us sit in and on the huge fire trucks, adorned with their fire helmets. None of these family excursions cost a cent to get in, and lasting memories were instilled in all of us. As a result of these learning experiences, when I had children I took them once a week to a zoo or museum to expand their knowledge of life and the world.

A new resort opened on 114th Street. Mom and Dad bought us a pool for the backyard. It was about four-by-four feet square, about two feet deep, if that, and had a small, triangular wooden seat on each corner. It became the neighborhood cooling spot. Everybody came over in their bathing suits to the Uptons' backyard. Dad held the baby, my brothers were splashing and having fun, and we girls and our friends were there in our bathing caps. We didn't have to worry about our hair getting wet or getting water in our ears—we were lucky we got our feet wet! When all else failed, we turned on the hose!

Trips to Coney Island are my first memory of a beach where we went in the ocean and played in the sand. The Cyclone roller coaster, Wonder Wheel, Parachute jump, and Steeplechase were big attractions. Rockaway Beach is where we went quite often, baby carriage and all. We took the Crossbay Boulevard bus or the Liberty Avenue el to Beach 116, the last stop for both. Traveling on the train, we used to see houses on stilts in the water in Broad Channel and wondered how people could live there. There were shabby wooden "summer cottages" for rent on Beach 116 by the boardwalk. They looked like shacks to me, as if a match would devour them in a minute. Some families rented them to vacation on the shore. Beach 116 was a popular, crowded, busy thoroughfare. I called it "blanket city." because you had to be cautious not to step on someone, or their belongings, when heading for the water.

We usually sat back near the boardwalk and played in the sand with pails and shovels. Our bathing suits were nothing fancy—usually Mom's or oversized hand-me-downs. We all stayed together and could only go near or in the water if Mom or Dad were there. We usually all got sunburns, because there were no precautions taken in the '40s and '50s to protect your skin.

We all looked so healthy with our sunburned complexions—and eventual freckles. Dad enjoyed the beach, and Mom hated it, but she never showed her disdain. She couldn't swim, which is why she made sure all of us learned. Knowing we all loved the beach, Mom would sacrifice and take all of us by herself to Rockaway and sit in the sand by the water, covered with a towel, in total vigilance as we went in the water. One time she panicked when she couldn't see Dennis. Suddenly a lifeguard, an older man, approached Mom with Dennis in tow. He said Dennis was tumbling in the waves and struggling to get up. Mom was so grateful as she hugged Dennis that I thought she was going to cry. Through the years Mom avoided the sun by using an umbrella. When we attended baseball games that my brothers were in, you could spot Mom a mile away—the only umbrella to be seen on a hot, dry summer day. Her efforts paid off; she always had beautiful skin.

Sometimes we went to Rockaway Beach on a Sunday afternoon and just walked along the boardwalk as a family. We were in our Sunday best, and Mom and Dad always looked so nice holding hands and enjoying being with each other. The aroma of cotton candy and popcorn filled the air. The sweltering heat carried the voices of the vendors, sweating as they plodded through the hot sand shouting, "Ices here! Ice creams here! Cold soda here! Get'cha nice cold ices, ice cream, sodas." We usually ended up at Playland on 98th Street having fun on a few of the nickel and dime rides, getting a drink or ice cream as a treat, and taking the train back home. During the summer there were weekly fireworks at Rockaway. We'd take the train to the 98th Street station, stand on the platform to watch the dazzling display, then cross over to the platform on the opposite side and go home. All for one fare!

We also went to Camp Bishop McDonell in Commack for a two-week vacation paid for by the St. Vincent de Paul Society and run by the Daughters of Wisdom nuns. It was a treat for the poor city kids, and I guess we qualified. My mother took us into Sutphin Boulevard, Jamaica, where all the children gathered to take the Long Island Railroad to Commack, where a bus picked us up and took us to camp. Camp Bishop McDonell was acres of wide open, spacious greenery. There was a large grassy area with a flag pole and some benches in the center. This was surrounded by three buildings on the left and three buildings and a chapel on the right. We were in the "F" building next to the chapel. Each of the buildings was simple—wooden, long, and narrow—and had cots on each side for us kids. A small room in the rear was where the nun in charge slept, and the clicking of her rosary beads told us when she was up and about. There was a huge, open dining area with wooden benches and tables a short distance from the cottages. The building was wooden, with a four-foot wall around it, with supporting beams that connected it with the roof, allowing the air to come through. Part of the building was the bathrooms and showers, which had ice-cold water all the time.

Just like home, every day we had to make our beds and the nun would check to make sure all was neat and clean. Each morning we all went outside in the grassy area to say morning prayers, salute the flag as it was raised, and sing the national anthem. Then we had breakfast, where we got in line to get our food. One time there was orange marmalade, and I hated it. It made me gag. The nun made me sit there all day long until I ate it. I wasn't clever enough then to toss it on the dirt floor or somehow get rid of it. I sat there through lunch and dinner, couldn't go out and play, and finally the nun took the marmalade away after a lecture about wasting food. Each day ended on the grassy area with a prayer and the taking down of the flag.

The open field where we played was great and had the biggest sliding pond I ever saw. It seemed about ten feet wide, so a whole bunch of us could go down it at once. There were lots of swings and a spinning wheel that you pushed with your feet and hopped on for a ride. The nuns watched us like hawks, and boy, were they tough! Lorraine once took a slug of water from a fountain, swished it around in her mouth, and spit it out. One of the nuns, probably sweltering from the starch of her habit, ran over and yanked Lorraine's hair so hard she was crying for a long time. I hope the nuns had a short memory span, because ironically, Jeri and Lorraine ended up attending Our Lady of Wisdom High Academy in Ozone Park, where these nuns taught.

We made a few trips by bus to Sunken Meadow beach, which was always an adventure. There were no major roads then, and the ride was scenic. We'd sing songs—"Do your ears hang low, do they wobble to and fro …"—and have fun as the bus bounced over dirt roads shadowed by many beautiful trees. There was no boardwalk at Sunken Meadow then, but the beach on the Long Island Sound was—and still is—filled with stones and rocks and was murder on the feet. The nuns watched carefully as we all splashed and swam in the refreshing water in the bathing suits they supplied. On the trip back to camp, the bus was filled with jubilant, tired, sandy children after an exhilarating day at the beach. Take a shower! Time for supper! After dinner, sometimes we would gather to sit on the benches by the cottages and watch a movie. The best part of the two weeks was when we'd get a letter from Mom and Dad, saying how they missed us. We sent postcards home, and evidently Mom kept them, because I read them recently. Even though camp was fun, I was anxious to be back home with my younger brothers; I missed them terribly. When the two weeks at camp were over, Mom met us at the train station in Jamaica, and it felt so good to be home again. Boys went for the next two weeks to camp, and as the oldest and only boy at the time, it must have been a little scary for George to go alone. By the time my younger brothers went to camp, there was a swimming pool on the campsite. They kept track of each other, but in most cases didn't like staying there two weeks.

When I was young, my parents very wisely bought property in a place called Ronkonkoma. It was when Long Island was all potato farms and dirt roads. When a trip there was planned, Mom was up half the night cooking fried chicken and making salads and sandwiches and plenty to drink for all of us. We would take the LIRR—baby stroller and all—to the Lake Ronkonkoma station and walk the dirt roads quite a distance to "our" property, passing a summer bungalow or two along the way. The property was marked off with baby food jars (I wonder why!) that were buried in the dirt in a corner of the "Upton Estate." Once discovered, we proceeded to have a picnic, climb the trees, play ball, play hide-and-seek and tag, and have a great time. We all kept an eye on the little ones. A few bumps and bruises occurred, but mostly laughter could be heard. Then we'd pack up, rebury the baby food jars, and take the train home. We were tired, sweaty, dusty with dirt and sand—but oh so happy! Through the years, our various family adventures to the city and to the country gave all of us an appreciation of both.

Chapter 7

Of course, using the single bathroom in our house was a true test of patience—and bladder control. There was always a line. George still took forever to fix his slick pompadour, making those in line more vocal and jittery. And this is where the *milk bottle* came into play. It seems my younger brothers always waited until the last minute when Mother Nature called, so an empty milk bottle was placed in the pantry entrance next to the bathroom for their convenience. The milk bottle sure helped shorten the line for the bathroom! Of course responsibility to empty and clean the "glass potty" was left to us older sisters, but it beat cleaning up a puddle! There was no time wasted piddling around! To this day, whether I'm in line in the supermarket, ladies room, movie, or restaurant, I entertain people by telling them to be patient, that I came from a family of twelve, and spent half my life in line—waiting for breakfast, lunch, dinner, and the bathroom. It usually eases the tension and puts a few smiles on the waiting faces.

Which brings up a subject that has always baffled me I've seen guys toss a basketball across the court and get it in; baseball players hit a ball on target and get a home run; golfers hit a ball and get it in the hole that is hundreds of yards away. How come, when in a bathroom, males keep missing the large opening that is the toilet? As a sister, a mother, an aunt, and a grandmother, I would like to suggest that when little boys are being potty trained, they be given extra lessons—in target practice!

Naturally, as time passed, we were all advancing in age and school. George, who was always very smart, wanted to be an architect and attended Brooklyn Tech High School, where he did very well. He was tall like Dad and was really getting into the social scene. He started going to dances held at the church and still enjoyed his display of Lionel Trains, which was set up in the basement. He was always reading, very often still in bed under the blankets with a flashlight. Dolores matured into a beautiful young lady. She was a smart, pretty, five-foot-two blonde and a good dancer. She was very popular and had a lot of friends. She started attending Dominican Commercial High School to become a secretary. She was always helping Mom and became like a second mom to some of us. Reenie, Jeri, Lorraine, and I were still in St. Bennies. I wanted to be like Dolores—except I kept growing taller!

In the '40s and '50s, there was an unspoken prejudice about different nationalities, which seemed to be part of everyone's upbringing. Families from various countries came through Ellis Island, settled in New York City, and naturally lived near other immigrants from their native country. Irish Town, Little Italy, German Town, China Town, etc., were all safe havens for the new arrivals who spoke the same language. Somewhere along the way all were categorized. "The Irish are drunks," "the Italians are Mafia," and "Germans are cold and unfeeling." When I asked my mom about this, she just said, "People are people, no matter where they come from. There are good and bad people in all." One time while walking home from school with an Italian friend, we were laughing and kidding around, and I said, "Oh, you silly guinea you." I didn't know that was a bad word, and she really got mad and called me "A lousy Mick." Well, I wasn't mad because I didn't know that was an insulting word either. We were all raised with certain prejudices. In time we all learned to ignore the put-down slang words that were hurtful and meaningless. I am reminded, a la Mom's advice, that there are "good and bad people in all."

Mom felt the same way about different religions. She always said, "There is one God. Some call Him Allah, some call Him Jesus, others call Him Buddha—but there is one God who we all worship in different ways." Mom was ecumenical way before her time. She never talked about being Lutheran. Once I had a crush on a neighborhood boy who was not Catholic and asked Mom if that was okay. She told me it hurts sometimes when you can not practice your own faith in your own church, and it would be best for me to meet boys who were Catholic. At the time, I was too young to realize the depth of what she was saying but with maturity surmised how difficult it was for her to give up practicing her faith. For love of my father, she sacrificed attending Lutheran services, unquestionably raised twelve Catholic children, and never, ever suggested it was painful. She was a woman born before her time and through the years presaged world events. She very often said during conflicts with Russia that it wasn't Russia we had to worry about, and that someday it would be the United States and Russia united against China, the "Sleeping Bear." She always believed that the Catholic church was one of the strongholds of our nation and a leader in setting societal ethics and morals. She often said that if the Catholic church started to waiver and weaken, all of society would be affected. She believed in and repeated these warnings about China and the Catholic church many times through the years. I am forever thankful for a mother who was ecumenical in her beliefs and blessed with foresight and wisdom beyond our times.

In school I was always at the end of the line for everything because of my height. The boys all seemed about two feet tall. My father's family members said I looked like Aunt Marion. Well, Aunt Marion was a very kind, caring, loving woman, but I saw pictures of her when she was growing up—tall and skinny—and she looked like Popeye's Olive Oyl. And she was never married! Not for nothing, but what kind of future was I looking at? And then there was my mother's family, who were all short. My mother's brother, Uncle Erich, was married to Aunt Mary, who spoke in a very shrill, high-pitched voice, and usually tactlessly blurted out whatever was on her mind. Every time she saw me, she would put her hand on her cheek, and shriek, "My God, Vera, she's getting so tall! She's so skinny! What's the matter with her? Her feet are so big! What size shoe does she wear?" Blah, blah, blah. Needless to say I felt like a freak and figured I was destined to work in the circus or enter the convent. My mother would just keep telling me to stand up straight, don't slouch, and keep my shoulders back. My five-foot-two mom constantly reminded me, and all my brothers and sisters, about standing tall and erect for good posture. No slouching allowed!

CHAPTER 8

Moving to 114th Street meant walking to and from school with new friends. I walked home a lot with Jeannette, who was blonde, pretty, and fun to be with. In fifth grade, a new girl moved in around the corner on 115th Street and was in my class. We started to walk home together from school and go to each other's houses. Her name was Frances Q. She was pretty, had black hair, and was tall like me, and I was so glad we became friends. My parents weren't too crazy about Fran; they thought she was too nervy and pushy. And that's what I liked about her! She was different. She had a collection of butterflies and was very much into insects, which was not my bag at all. One time we were sleeping in a tent in her yard, and I saw this slimy glob. It was a slug, and I ran screaming out of the tent, while she was examining it and naming its species. *Yuck!*

Fran liked coming to my house because there was always something going on, and I liked her house because it was quieter. Her father, Joe, was an insurance man, worked out of the house, and used to take Fran and me for rides to the beach. Mr. Q, a tall, handsome man, sat reflectively on the beach while we collected shells and dug up sand crabs. Mrs. Q—Terri—was a pretty, slim, demure lady. She used to say that Fran and I complimented each other because she had dark hair and mine was light and we were both tall. I was so thankful for a tall friend! Mrs. Q was mild tempered and very creative and taught us to make paper mache puppets and other things.

She was much more lenient than her husband, who really laid down the law, and used to get mad at some of the things Fran and I did—like the time he saw us on the grated cement center of Atlantic Avenue. As the LIRR trains passed below, we stood over the grated air vents to catch the breeze, the cool air going right up our clothes to our hair. Mr. Q pulled his car over, and told us to "get the hell home." He read us the riot act! Good thing he didn't see us when Mom sent me to the store for a fifty-pound bag of potatoes. We put it in the carriage, covered it with a baby blanket, and would stop and yell, "Shut up, you little brat." and whack the potatoes. People looked, shook their heads, but nobody said boo. We thought it was pretty funny and laughed. In today's world, we'd get in trouble. But for what—hitting a potato in the eye? We used to go down Fran's basement, play some seventy-eight records or the radio, use a broom handle, put a tin can on top, and pretend it was our microphone. We'd make up skits and routines like we were on the stage. And we always practiced the Lindy, a popular dance then. We thought we were hot stuff.

Sometimes, for lack of anything to do, we sat at her father's desk and made phone calls to people, pretending we were someone else. There was a stuck-up boy in our class who lived in the back section of an apartment house. We called, got his father, and said we represented the electric company. Explaining that there were electrical problems in the area, we asked if he would check to see if the streetlights were on in the front of his building. He said he'd check, ran down to the front of the building, and got back on the phone to say yes, the lights were on. We thanked him and said, "Good—now blow them out"! Then we hung up and laughed ourselves silly.

Fran and I behaved well in school and did our homework and everything we were supposed to do, and yet when our parents went up for interviews with the nuns, the story was different. My parents were told that Fran was a bad influence on me, and her parents were told I was a bad influence on Fran. *Impossible!*

Neither of us was a bad person. We weren't hoody, didn't smoke, didn't curse or swear, but together maybe we were a little "curious, creative, and mischievous." That's all. Once in seventh grade, we both got a 79% average on our report card and stood on the corner of 115th Street and 95th Avenue until the sun was going down. Fran's mother was much more lenient and tolerant than mine, but I didn't know if I'd live to see the sun rise the next day. My sentence was no friends, no TV, and more studying until my grades improved. Education and good grades came *first!*

Against all odds, Fran and I continued to be friends, and it was somewhere around seventh or eighth grade when we went to Kressges, the five and dime store, to buy our first bras. Her mother measured us and told us how to buy a bra and what size to get. Fran was ready for one, but I wasn't. I just couldn't find a bra with an A-minus cup! Still can't! The bra probably cost about $1. We wanted nothing but the best! Watch out world—we're growing up!

Easter was a very special occasion in our house. Mom would take us shopping to Goodwin's basement in Jamaica or Klein's at Union Square for a new outfit. We'd usually top it off with a straw hat, pretty gloves, and a purse from Kressges, Grants, or Woolworth's. New patent leather shoes, if needed, were bought in Miles or National shoe stores. Mom bought taps for the shoes so they would last longer. After finding our hidden Easter baskets, we'd all get dressed for Mass. Dad would sit on the couch as we all lined up in front of him for approval. One by one, we all passed inspection as Daddy told us how nice we looked. He told all his daughters they were beautiful, and we felt it, because Daddy said so. Easter candies were devoured all day, along with the leg of lamb or ham dinner for the special occasion. Daddy took movie pictures of us and our friends with a new eight-millimeter camera, which had four big, hot light bulbs for indoor use. Aunt Julie and

Uncle Herb usually gave us chocolate candy, which was a treat, especially since it was what we had "given up" for Lent.

Lent was, and still is, a sacrificial time in the Catholic church, ending with Holy Thursday, Good Friday, Holy Saturday, and Easter. It was suggested, for whatever reason, that you visit three different churches on Holy Thursday. Fran and I decided, with parental permission, to ride our bikes to nine churches. We mapped out our route, put on our pedal pushers, and wore an inverted sailor hat, brim down, which was covered with decorative pins from various baseball teams, high schools, and organizations. We thought we were cool, packed a lunch, and took off! We pedaled to various churches in Richmond Hill, Ozone Park, S. Ozone Park, Jamaica, and Brooklyn. We ate our lunch in 102nd Street park, and discussed the difference in all the churches. Some were elaborately adorned, while others were simple in décor. It was after visiting St. Anthony of Padua that my pant leg got caught in the bike chain, and I couldn't move. How would we get home? Scared and nervous, we yanked, pulled, felt like crying, and finally freed my pant leg. Tired after our long trek, we got home feeling pretty proud of ourselves for visiting nine churches. Plus, I think we were hoping for forgiveness and extra blessings from God for the pranks we pulled.

We always rode our bikes around the neighborhood with some friends and of course were a little boy-crazy by this time. We would nonchalantly just "happen" to ride down the street where some boys lived, and Bobby H. and Billy K. joined us. Billy K. liked Fran, but he had this habit of riding past her and snapping the back of her bra. Boy, was she mad! She kept telling him to stop, but he'd sneak up behind her and do it again. She was so angry, embarrassed, and insulted, and we just biked to her house and talked about it all the way home. It just wasn't right for him to do that, so we decided to take matters into our own hands. The two of us sat down at her father's desk and wrote a letter—an anonymous, unsigned letter—to Billy K.'s mom, informing her of what a jerk her son was and that he was a bra snapper. We also wrote an anonymous letter to Mrs. H. telling her that she shouldn't let her son Bobby hang around with Billy K. because he was a jerk and not a nice person. Boy, did we feel good and so self-righteous as we stamped and mailed the anonymous letters.

A few days later, I got to school early and went in the side entrance of the school. When I opened the door, I could have died! Sister James Immaculate, our eighth grade teacher, was with Mrs. K., who was angry and talking a mile a minute. Sr. James Immaculate, with downcast eyes, pointed at me and told me in a veeerrrrry slow, deep voice, "Stand against the wall." I thought, "Oh my God, they're gonna shoot me!" Mrs. K. was going on and on, and I just wanted to cry because I knew my mother would kill me for getting into trouble. Then Fran came in and was told to join me against the wall. I started to cry, and Fran poked me and said, "Knock it off, Upton, we didn't do anything wrong." Finally, Mrs. K left. Sister James Immaculate (Jamsie was her student given nickname)—who was tough—told us she was ashamed of us and that we were both in a lot of trouble. Again, she spoke with downcast eyes as we the sinners stood before her. The three of us then walked upstairs in silence to the classroom.

A short while later, Sister called us up to her desk and told us to go over to the church—the priest was waiting for us. Fran was unruffled, and I was petrified. So Laverne and Shirley went to the church. The priest instructed us that we had to go to confession for what we did. When I entered the confessional, I thought for sure the wall would collapse this time and the ever-burning flames of hell would take me right down there. The priest proceeded to tell me that writing an anonymous letter was a very serious sin, and I was headed for a life of crime. Fran got the same message. I then recited a heartfelt act of contrition and went to the altar to do my penance—one hundred Our Fathers, one hundred Hail Mary's, and one hundred Glory Be's. This time I made sure to do the math right.

Fran and I nervously walked home for lunch. Mom didn't say anything, and I was never so glad we didn't have a phone. I was relieved none of my siblings were sent home with a note for Mom. When I got back to class, Sister asked me if I told my mother what happened, and of course I said yes. (I was scared, not stupid!) She asked me what my mother said, and I told her she was very ashamed of me. And that was it! Fran and I still talk about it sometimes and laugh that it didn't take anyone too long to figure out it was us who wrote the anonymous letters. I wonder why? We figure the nuns had the letter, hung it in the convent kitchen, and probably had a good laugh over it themselves. In today's society, Billy K. would have been in a lot of trouble for doing what he did, not us. At a St. Bennie's reunion a few years ago, I saw Billy K. and had to struggle to keep a straight face. He was with his mother.

CHAPTER 9

Something that was heard about, whispered about, but never discussed openly was *it—sex*. Mom and Dad had a lot of kids, but I knew nothing about what caused them. My friends and I would talk and wonder about something called a "period" that girls were supposed to get. Everything was kept secret in those days. Fran's mother had books around the house that she encouraged us to read that were about *it,* but I felt embarrassed and thought it was wrong and sinful. One friend who got her period thought it was from red cabbage she had eaten; another girl's mother slapped her face and said, "Now you're a woman." My mother shoved a sanitary napkin through the bathroom door and said, "You'll get it once a month." But nobody—I mean nobody—explained what *it* was, or what was happening. We weren't told it was a natural part of growing up or that our bodies were preparing for adulthood and possible motherhood. I realize now that Mom and a lot of women then grew up in the secretiveness of the times and just didn't know themselves what was happening. How could Mom explain something that she herself didn't really know about? Knowledge of body parts and functions were not talked about, and the subject of having babies was taboo. But *it* remained a source of conversation and curiosity for most of us growing up then.

Naturally because Mrs. Upton had five very responsible daughters, we all eventually became the babysitters of the neighborhood. We could baby-sit on weekends, but not much during the week because school work came first. The rate then was 25¢ or 50¢ an hour. After school, I also cleaned the house two days a week for a working couple who lived next door. They knew the Upton girls had plenty of house-cleaning experience! I vacuumed, dusted, and scrubbed the whole place from top to bottom. After a few months of housecleaning, Mom said I should ask for a raise, told me what to do and say, and I was paid more money. That's where the *chutzpa* comes from! Whatever I made I gave to Mom and was allowed to keep some spending money. Every week I went to a record shop on Atlantic Avenue (I really think it was a bookie joint) and bought the latest seventy-eight hit record for $1. The Platters were big in my collection. Mom put the rest of my earnings in my savings account and showed me the passbook and the interest that was accumulating. Rockefellers—watch out!

I don't know when the relationship started, but we had a family doctor who lived on Euclid Avenue in Brooklyn. Dr. Ralph was a compassionate man who made house calls, as most doctors did in those days. He was fortyish, small of stature, Jewish, and spoke with a German-like accent. When we were sick, Mom took us by bus to his office, which always had a strong medicine smell. He would examine each of us, give us a shot of penicillin, give Mom medicine to take home for us, and charge her $2. He was obviously aware of the financial struggle. He used to tell us stories from the past about people who had died in the streets of diphtheria and how helpless he felt. He had a car to make house calls. I'll never forget when he came to our house by bus in a real bad snowstorm. Mom was sick and had passed out. Dad was frantic with concern and looked like he was going to cry when Dr. Ralph showed up, covered in snow, with his black doctor's bag. To this day I don't know what was wrong with Mom, but Dr. Ralph kept quietly muttering, "Very sick woman. Very sick woman." Mom stayed in bed, and Grandma Wolf came over to take care of us kids, sometimes with Aunt Julia, who always made us Jell-O with fruit in it.

Fran and I continued being friends, which was helpful when I came home from the store and Mom discovered I was short-changed one, two, or three cents, which meant returning to the store by bike or on foot. With Fran just around the corner, all I did was go to her house, ask her mom for the pennies, and kill time until I went home with the "change from the store." Fran went on a lot of family outings with us. She pitched in and helped carry things, push the stroller, or whatever there was to do. We didn't have the money to go away on vacation, so we started taking family day trips up the Hudson River by boat. Mom would be up all night making the chicken and salads. We all helped to make the sandwiches, pack some snacks and goodies, and of course had tons of milk and juices to take. It was hard to fall asleep because we were all excited about the boat ride.

Daddy brought boxes home from work, and we all helped pack the food and drinks for the trip. We older girls got dressed quick and then took care of the younger ones. We dressed the boys, made sure they ate breakfast, went to the bathroom, and were ready to leave. The baby was fed (there was *always* a baby), the baby food and bottles were packed, and whatever didn't fit in the stroller was carried by each of us.

Walking as fast as we could to catch the Lefferts Boulevard bus to Kew Gardens, we'd then take the subway to 42nd Street. We'd hurriedly walk to the west side piers and board one of two steam ships—the *Peter Stuyvesant* or the *Alexander Hamilton*. Settling in on the outer deck, the ship would start rolling up the Hudson to Indian Point. As usual, Mom and Dad would just about sit down, and somebody was hungry or thirsty already. The baby and the younger ones stayed with Mom and Dad, and Fran and I and my sisters were allowed to walk around the boat, as long as we stayed together. We saw the sweaty crew members shoveling coal into the furnace of the ship to get up steam. There was an open area and a juke box, and Fran and I would dance the lindy and have a ball in our "cool" pedal pushers. We took turns leading and following to "Hound Dog" and "Don't be Cruel" by Elvis.

Mom and Dad relaxed on the deck chairs, always sitting close and holding hands. Dad would put his arm around Mom, and they seemed not only to enjoy being with each other, but also watching their children have fun. With Dad working two full-time jobs, their rare time together was fully appreciated. We knew when we were approaching Indian Point, because on the opposite side of the Hudson we could see the retired "mothball fleet." which were the war ships that fought during World War II. It was always fun watching as the ship pulled into the pier to let everyone off and then pulled away to continue on to Bear Mountain and West Point.

Indian Point—which today is the site of a nuclear power plant—was very pretty and had a lot of grassy knolls that we just loved to roll down. There were plenty of picnic tables, and we usually chose one under a shady tree. We girls would help Mom put out the food and drinks, and we'd all fill ours and the boys' plates, which were real dishes from home, not paper. Dolores, Reenie, Jeri, Lorraine, Fran, and I would split the chores of washing the dishes and silverware under a nearby faucet, repacking the food for the next surge, or taking the boys to the bathroom. Then we'd climb the plentiful trees, play tag, and have a baseball game. We always brought a ball and bat! Mom and Dad usually pitched, and the bases would be a tree, a rock, or a bench. Everybody got a chance at bat, even the little ones.

Often there was a traveling amusement show at Indian Point,

and we'd go on all the rides, ending up with an ice cream treat. Then, while the boys ran around playing, climbing trees, and rolling down the hills, we'd set the table and finish the remaining food for supper. Sandwiches and drinks were still available for the boat ride home. We had less to carry on the train and bus, and we tiredly fell asleep with dreams of a wonderful day. Eventually the annual boat rides were taken to Bear Mountain, where we swam in the huge pool and walked through the zoo. One time we missed the boat at 42nd Street and Dad hailed cabs to take us to Harlem, the next and last pier of departure. We made it!

Then we started taking boat rides from Battery Park in downtown Manhattan up to Rye Beach on the Long Island Sound, which beyond a doubt became everyone's favorite place. It was beautifully landscaped with a well-maintained colorful floral display throughout the spacious park. We didn't spend a lot of time playing ball there, because there were rides, rides, rides for all to enjoy. Ray and Eddie took good care of Dennis and Robert on the rollercoaster, after shooting at each other from their chain-held flying airplanes. Through the years, as family automobiles became available, Rye Beach became the amusement park of choice for the whole family. Once we missed the boat to Rye Beach and ended up taking a boat trip to Keansburg Beach, New Jersey. A new destination, a new adventure—another fun day!

January 16, 1955, was my 13th birthday. Fran organized a surprise birthday party for me, which was held in the basement of a classmate, Richard. Rock and Roll was just hitting the music scene, and we lindied to Bill Haley and the Comets' "Shake, Rattle & Roll", "Dim, Dim the Lights," and a lot of other great songs. Since roller skating was popular at the time, the whole class chipped in and surprised me with a pair of white leather roller skates and an aqua metal carrying case. Many a Saturday afternoon was spent at Hillside Roller Rink. Fran's father often drove us to the Old 1938 World's Fair building in Flushing Meadow, which had two rinks—one for roller skating and the other for ice skating. The cost was .15 cents for each rink. We loved doing both and wore our short skating skirts as we glided around the rinks. Mom and Dad were happy to see us being active and out of trouble.

January 1955 was the graduation from St. Bennies for the students who were six months ahead of us. We heard one of the boys we knew, Bobby H., was having a graduation party on Sunday afternoon, and Fran and I couldn't understand why we weren't invited. Dressed in our Sunday finery, we moseyed past his house and saw a lot of people inside. We were surprised, felt a little hurt, and didn't know what to do. So we decided to have a catch. Fran stood at the end of a driveway, and I stood on the opposite side of the street at the end of a driveway facing her. Vigorously swinging our arms, we went through the motions of throwing and catching—but we didn't have a ball! Lo and behold, Mrs. H. suddenly appeared (probably after getting phone calls from the neighbors) and invited us in. Of course, we shyly responded as if totally surprised by her invitation but did go in to find a house full of Bobby's relatives. We met his family, had some goodies, and were relieved we weren't "left out" of a friend's party. Whatever we did, it worked—nobody got in trouble, and we had a good time!

To prepare for our upcoming June graduation, we had to take entrance exams to various high schools. I loved fixing and curling hair and wanted to be a beautician. Mom wouldn't hear of such a lowly endeavor, so beauty school was out. I also always wanted to be a model, because some people said I'd be good at it since I was tall and skinny. Modeling was totally out of the question!

Mom said there was *no way* any daughter of hers was going to walk around in her underwear in front of some dirty old men. So, even though mine were bigger, I followed in Dolores's footsteps and was accepted at Dominican Commercial High School in Jamaica. The day the letter of acceptance arrived, Fran yelled through the yard from 115th Street that she was accepted too. We were both ecstatic, and our parents probably cringed at the thought. We first had to take New York State Regent's exams under very strict guidelines. No talking, no looking around, no cheating, no bathrooms! We were allowed to breathe—and had to sign "I do so declare …" as an oath of honesty. We passed! We were ready to graduate!

It was a wonderful experience to receive a diploma. St. Bennie's church was filled with the graduates' happy relatives, the altar adorned with beautiful flowers, as we walked into the church to the sounds of organ music set in an aura of pomposity. I felt so pretty and grown up in the dress Mom and I picked out, especially when Dad pinned a beautiful corsage on it. All nine of my brothers and sisters were there, dressed in suits and dresses, right down to 2 year-old Robert. A very special day was shared with my family and my best friend.

Fran's parents gave her permission to have a "boy/girl" graduation party. Most of the kids invited were in our class, along with a few boys from the previous January class. We were a really clean-cut, nice group of young teenagers, all decked out in our fancy dresses and suits, as we danced in the living and dining rooms. For the fast songs, the girls usually danced together, and the boys sat there like lumps. Mrs. Q sat quietly in the living room, watching everyone like a hawk—especially when we danced the slow ones. A favorite that year was "Unchained Melody" by Al Hibbler. It was a great party. After everyone left,

Mr. Q was furious to discover the aftermath of the gathering. Someone had thrown eggs behind the refrigerator, twisted and broken a window screen, and believe it or not, peed in the bathtub and his hair tonic. He was ranting and raving about finding who did this, and Mrs. Q tried to calm him down and said she would call the parents.

The following day Mrs. Q phoned all the boys' parents. In her usual calm and dignified manner, she informed the parents that "someone urinated" in the hair tonic and bathtub and set a time for all the boys to come to the house. They all showed up and stood nervously at the bottom of the stairs as Mrs. Q informed them her husband would be right down. Fran and I were sitting quietly in the living room, waiting for the axe to fall. Mr. Q, a big, very hairy man who wore sleeveless undershirts with thin shoulder straps, was in the middle of shaving. He came barreling down the stairs in his undershirt, half his face covered in shaving cream, wielding and waving his razor, bellowing, "Okay, guys, who the hell pissed in the tub?" You had to be there. Mrs. Q looked mortified, and Fran and I were hysterically laughing into the couch pillows. I think maybe the boys had to go home and change their underwear. We found out years later at a class reunion that the culprit was Tommy M. He was lucky they didn't use DNA samples then!

During the summer of 1955 we found out that a fellow graduate, Richard, was diagnosed with polio, a much-dreaded disease at the time. It was in Richard's basement where my surprise birthday party was held. Polio was a devastating disease that caused paralysis of the spine and affected all motor skills. There was talk that it was contagious and could possibly be gotten by swimming in public pools. That meant no more swimming at Cypress Hill's pool near city line. The public was in a near-panic regarding polio, and thank God a polio vaccine was discovered and administered to all children and young adults nationwide. Richard, a very nice, handsome young man from a loving family, was in everyone's prayers, and is now in the gentle arms of Jesus.

1955 was also the year my mother's favorite brother, Erich, died from stomach cancer. Cancer was known to be a life-taking disease and feared by everyone. Mom was totally devastated and heartbroken and cried for days in anguish. Uncle Erich was married to Aunt Mary, and they had three sons—Freddy, Erich, and Kurtis. Cousin Erich was a young teenager when his father died, and he and I have remained close through the years. Erich recently told me that Aunt Vera—my Mom—was the only person in the family who was always there for someone in need or trouble. Whether it was sickness, death, divorce, or a family problem, she was there to speak openly and offer advice, trying to help ease the pain and help resolve the situation. It was her nature to be there for others.

Fran and I had to go into Jamaica to be measured for our uniforms for Dominican Commercial High School. They were brown and tan and must have been designed by a woman hater. Whatever size you were measured, the uniform was made larger. After all, we didn't want the world to know that Catholic girls had shapes! The uniform was topped off—or bottomed out—with an ugly pair of lace-up brown oxford shoes. When getting off the bus, the boys would yell, "There's the brownies in their Maidenform shoes." When school started in September, Fran and I took the Atlantic Avenue bus from 114th Street, which dropped us off right outside the school in Jamaica. There were other students on the bus going to various public schools. We had no choice but to sit near the front, because the rear of the bus was taken over by the girls who went to Jamaica Vocational. They got on the bus before us in Ozone Park, and they were *tough!* We ignored their comments about our uniforms, tried not to listen to their cursing and swearing, and probably would have ridden on the roof if they told us to.

Dominican Commercial was an all-girls Catholic school with an excellent reputation for graduating well-prepared secretaries. Tuition was $17.50 a month at the time. The Sisters of St. Dominic, our teachers, were a much happier order of nuns than we had in St. Bennies. They were friendly, open, and more outgoing, even though they too wore the long white habits, black veils, and starch. High school was a whole new experience. There were over three hundred new freshmen, and we were all broken down into different classes. Fran and I were in the same class. We changed classes sometimes and were monitored in the hallways by members of the Leo Honor Society, the goody-two-shoes. They wore black bands on their arms and reported any troublemakers to the principal. My sister Dolores—then a senior—was a high-ranking student and Leo Honor member.

Dominican Commercial girls were not allowed to wear makeup. I myself was questioned about my blonde hair. Blonde hair, which starts out almost white sometimes, tends to darken with each passing year. Mom liked our blonde hair, which was getting drab and mousy, and she encouraged Dolores and me to lighten our hair with peroxide. One nun went eyeball to eyeball with me and asked if I bleached my hair. I just said I was born with blonde hair. *Phew!* Eventually I met Miss Clairol and a "deeply rooted" lifetime friendship was formed.

For four years, all I heard from the nuns was, "You're nothing like your sister." I wanted to say, "No kidding! For one thing I'm about five inches taller than her!" But I didn't. Demerits were given out for any misbehavior, and it didn't take me long to get started on them. Nothing serious—I just did some silly, goofy stuff. Our freshman home room teacher said if she heard one more peep in the room, a demerit would be given. Of course I said "Peep." was called to her desk, and was given my first demerit. I had to fill it out and write the reason for the demerit. I just wrote "for peeping." So how serious can that be? But I was still glad we didn't have a telephone at home.

Another time in English class we each had to stand in front of the class and give a recitation. One classmate was always shy and nervous and used to break out in hives when called upon. For some reason, even though I was tall I was seated in the front row. When this classmate got up to give her presentation, I tore off some black binding from the then marbleized notebook and put it on my front teeth. As she was speaking and looking around, I smiled at her in this toothless way. Ping! Ping! Ping! The red hives appeared like clockwork. "Miss Upton, go down to the principal's office!" resounded in the room. I went to the office of Sister Dorothy, who was busy writing. She looked up quickly and asked why I was there. I didn't say a word, displayed my black teeth—and she laughed hysterically! Funny or not, I still got a demerit.

One time I was in the school bathroom washing my hands at the sink, which was next to an open window overlooking the path the nuns used to get from school to the convent. In my haste, the bar of soap flew out of my hands, through the open window, and landed on the walkway two stories down. It was an accident, but there was no way I could retrieve it. I could have died the next day when I got to school and heard that one of the nuns slipped on a bar of soap and broke her leg while walking to the convent. I was scared to death, but knew I had to go to the principal's office and admit it was me who dropped the soap and somehow convince her it was an accident. I was ready to go and face the consequences when Marie, a fellow student with a sense of humor like mine, admitted she made up the story about the nun and the broken leg. She got me good, and I guess I got my payback for the hives stunt.

Since Fran loved animals, insects, and all sorts of species, we volunteered to clean the biology lab after school. Fran examined all the different specimens and one time took a chameleon out of its cage. It leaped out of her hand, took off, and got lost. For weeks I had the heebie jeebies every time we had biology. We used to poke around and look at everything, and one time I accidentally knocked over one of the plants. I went to clean it up, when I heard the clicking of a nun's rosary beads coming down the hall. I quick grabbed the dry mop, covered the plant, and moved it around slowly as if cleaning the floor. The nun looked in, very pleased, and said we were doing a good job. Phew! The black rags we were given to dust the furniture with, we realized, were the nuns' old stockings. We decided, instead of just shaking them out, to give them a good airing. We hung about ten of these black stockings out the second-floor biology room windows, closing the windows on the very top of them to hold them in place. We laughed ourselves silly watching the nuns' stockings blowing in the wind, dancing up a storm. The "DC Rockettes" were born, but never discovered! Thank God!

Being we were in high school, we were now entitled to go to Friday night Confraternity in St. Bennie's school auditorium. It started at eight o'clock with a religious talk by one of the priests, and then followed by a dance. If you weren't there for the priest's talk, you couldn't go in to dance, Catholic school kids included. Monsignor Hald, the pastor, was very concerned about not marring his highly polished auditorium floor, so we danced in the very rear, where the juke box was. Poodle skirts, ponytails, cardigan sweaters buttoned down the back, bobby socks, saddle shoes, and white bucks were bopping and moving to the beat of this new Rock and Roll music. A few of the boys were good dancers, but a lot of times the girls partnered to do the fast ones. I remember one guy who was a good fast dancer and would ask me to dance to what he called "my songs"—"Long Tall Sally" and "Boney Maroney." Now there's a real morale booster!

As busy as Mom was, she always took time to chaperone the dances and keep an eye on her daughters. As I got older, I realized no matter where any of us went, Mom was somehow going to show up. I'm sure she loved watching Dolores, who was popular and a great dancer. I wonder if she was chaperoning the night George met Peggy Joy, the girl he fell in love with and eventually married. When I danced a slow one with Tommy B, Mom said it looked like we were dancing on a dime, because we didn't move too much. "Blueberry Hill" by Fats Domino was a big hit, which Mom said had been a popular song when she was young and was considered sinful and risqué. "I found my thrill …" Boy, have times changed!

After Confraternity, many of us as a crowd would go to one of the nearby ice cream parlors. But this new fangled thing called "pizza" was becoming very popular. Russo's Pizza was near the church on Jerome Avenue and Lefferts Boulevard and was a little store front place with red-and-white plastic table cloths. A whole pizza pie cost $1 and was delicious! New to me, my first slice was scalding hot and the stretchy mozzarella cheese was never ending, to the point where I thought I was going to choke on it. Russo's is now quite an elegant catering hall and restaurant, well known for its great Italian food.

When Reenie started high school she didn't go to Confraternity much. She was smart, on the quiet side, kind of shy, always a lady, but really wasn't crazy about dancing or social events. When she was in eighth grade at St. Bennies, there was an upcoming graduation dance, which she never said anything about. One Friday night, the doorbell rang. I ran down to answer it, and there, to my surprise, stood a classmate of Reenie's dressed in a suit and tie with a corsage in hand. He was there to take Reenie to the dance! I invited the boy upstairs, quickly took Reenie into the bedroom, picked out a pretty dress for her to wear, did her hair in a nice 'do, and off they went! Reenie looked so pretty as she left—unexcitedly—wearing a beautiful corsage from her gentleman escort.

Reenie, a high-scoring student, was accepted at Bishop McDonnell Diocesan High School in Brooklyn. There was no tuition since it was for high achievers throughout the diocese. Uniforms were not worn, but a lady-like dress code was enforced. Jeri, who also was very smart, attended Our Lady of Wisdom Academy in Ozone Park, where uniforms were required. Both of them did very well and continued on to nursing schools. Wearing Catholic school uniforms was a big savings for Mom and Dad's budget, and an excellent education was achieved through their unending sacrifices. Education was a top priority, and they struggled and worked hard to make sure we got the best!

When we had dinner, or any meal, at home, we ate in shifts. We waited in line near the kitchen, and I often kid that there were times when total strangers probably came up the stairs, got in line, and were fed! For breakfast we usually had hot or cold cereals, eggs, pancakes or crepes, and French toast. Mom made a lot of big dinners due to the amount of mouths to feed. Meat, potatoes, and vegetables followed by Jell-O, pudding, or cake were the norm. Stews, pea soup, corn chowder, and potato soup were some choices. Sometimes we had lamb or pork chops, but Mom made a lot of roasts—meatloaf, beef, pork, etc.—and always with mashed potatoes and fresh vegetables. The potatoes and vegetables were peeled, scraped, and cut by us girls, and put into a huge pot for Mom—*only Mom*—to cook and mash. The stove and cooking were Mom's territory! (As Dolores got older, she was the *only* one allowed to help cook.) Usually there was delicious brown gravy to flavor everything.

Thinking I'd be finished quicker, I had the habit of mixing the vegetables and mashed potatoes together, and my brothers and sisters would yell, "Mom, she's doing that disgusting thing again!" Bacon, liver, and onions was a dish Mom and Dad loved and made often because it was full of iron and good for us. *Yuck* was a pretty common response to it from us kids. I smothered the liver with as many onions as I could to kill the taste. Usually on Friday (no meat allowed) we'd have fried apples or bananas, silvery smelts, grilled cheese, or fish cakes. Mom even made her own cheese pizzas! All of our meals included milk and *only* milk. Cavity-causing soda was taboo in our house. On St. Patrick's Day, of course, we had corned beef and cabbage. Mom put a very small glass by our plates, opened a bottle of beer, and allowed each of us to have about an inch to drink in celebration of our Irish heritage. Whatever we had for dinner was usually spiced with bickering over who was a Yankee or Brooklyn Dodger fan! I was a Dodger fan like Dad and sometimes went with him to Ebbets Field to watch a game—for .99 cents. Election time always brought up discussions of politics between Mom, a Republican, and Dad, a Democrat. No matter what the meal, Mom always made her freshly percolated coffee, which smelled soooooooo good. We all started drinking coffee in our teen years. All meals ended with us sweeping the floor, washing and drying the dishes, and a few arguments over whose turn it was to do what.

As we maturing daughters of George and Elvira Upton entered our teen years, we fell right in with the fad of very full, flared skirts that were the rage and required crinoline petticoats to keep them full. The crinoline slips had to be heavily starched to get the best effect. You should have seen our basement! It looked like a parasol convention! Once starched, we put our crinolines over opened umbrellas, chairs, boxes, and anything else we could find until they were dried stiff and worn again. When Dolores started working part-time after school, she started buying some real nice clothes, and I wanted to wear them too. We used to bicker a lot over clothes. One time I decided to "borrow" a skirt of hers. She was out on a date and wasn't available to ask her permission, which I suspected would have been denied. As I was walking down our street heading for a dance in one of her skirts, blossoming with crinolines, I could have died when she pulled up in a car with her date and saw me. I bolted! Looking back at the fact that Dolores was 5'2"and I was 5'7", I realize I probably invented the mini-skirt!

It took going to dances and social events to be introduced to the sarcasm and bantering that is part of growing up in New York City. Leaving a dance held at Dominican one night, I was thrilled—for a minute—when this boy came running up to me and said, "Did anyone ever tell you that you look like Lana Turner's sister? … Stomach"! I was so stunned I felt like crying, but caught on pretty quick. The next dance a boy came up and said, "Baby, baby, where ya been all my life?" I quickly responded, "Out of it, thank God." I felt so good inside that I had a sarcastic answer for him. I was getting the hang of it.

My parents didn't smoke (Dad did later in life), but smoking was something that it seemed a lot of people were into and was very accepted as part of "growing up." When my uncles were over to visit, I used to watch them as they lit their unfiltered cigarettes. As a young teen, curiosity got the better of me, and I took a "clippie" from the ashtray. I got a big wooden match from the kitchen and snuck in the bathroom to light the clippie, when there was a knock on the door. Mom said something spilled and she needed the clean-up rag. I quick opened the door slightly and shoved the rag out to her. Immediately there was another knock and Mom's deeper more serious voice saying, "Open that door!" I was sent to bed immediately. Since my father was working, Mom and George discussed what my punishment should be. George, who also smoked, thought I should be forced to eat a pack of cigarettes. (I wonder what the hospital would have charged to pump my stomach.) Lucky for me Mom didn't go for the idea, but I was restricted to the house for a while.

I had a friend who lived across the street and her family smoked a lot. They used to send her to the store for cigarettes and always told her to keep the change and buy ice cream or sodas for the two of us, which was a treat. Then one trip to the store she decided to buy another pack of cigarettes instead of a treat, and that's how the horrible habit of smoking started for both of us. There were no restrictions then, and no health warnings about smoking. The word was that it didn't look nice for girls to smoke and it stunted your growth. My sick joke about that is that maybe I would have been seven feet tall.

There were a lot of students at Dominican who smoked. *Shhhh!* Class was dismissed, uniform skirts were shortened by rolling up the waistband, normally forbidden lipstick and eye makeup were applied, and cigarettes were smoked. Peer pressure was strong to be one of the crowd. As the first female smoker in my family, I took a lot of whooping and punishment for doing so. Reenie was given permission to smoke, which my parents regretted doing because she smoked all the time. Jeri followed in pursuit, as did Lorraine and most of my brothers. Dolores never smoked.

Chapter 10

In the summer of 1956, I thought my world was crumbling. Fran's parents bought a house in Oakdale, *way* out on Long Island. I was devastated to think my best friend wasn't going to live nearby anymore. In September Fran and I started sophomore year, she at Seton Hall Academy and me at Dominican. Our friendship didn't end because we wrote letters back and forth all the time. All we wrote and talked about were *boys, boys,* and *boys*. Every day and every week it seemed each of us had a crush on somebody else.

In his travels as an insurance man, Mr. Q would pick me up and drive me to their new house for the weekend and often did the same in reverse, so Fran could stay at my house in Richmond Hill. Mr. Q usually had a "coff-a-cupee," as he jokingly called it, with Mom before driving home. Oakdale was truly the country then and didn't even have streetlights yet. I thought Fran's family was rich, because the ranch-styled house was so roomy and beautiful. We occupied ourselves by walking to town, passing a real old church with a cemetery and tombstones from the 17/1800s, when people died of the plague, consumption, etc. We often walked into Sayville and took the ferry to Fire Island for 50¢.

I thought Oakdale was beautiful, but Fran found it boring, with not much to do. She liked coming back to Richmond Hill to more familiar surroundings and people. I loved it when we spent weekends together. We still pulled off our usual pranks once in a while, aware that Mom was always watching. Like the time we told Mom we were going to the movies on a Saturday afternoon, when actually we were secretly meeting two boys who were taking us to the matinee. We were nervous, and as the picture started each of the boys put his arm around our shoulders. Scared stiff, we got up, said we were going to the ladies room, and ran like heck out of the movies. We ran for blocks as if being chased and finally stopped, caught our breath, and laughed our heads off. We were glad we got away from those two guys. How dare they get frisky and try to put their arms around us! One summer night, about nine o'clock, we asked Mom if we could go to Jahn's for ice cream. She said it was too late but we could go to the diner around the corner. Of course we went to Jahn's. While walking, we heard something and saw a man doing something indecent under the streetlight. Fran was mad because she forgot her glasses and couldn't see a darn thing! We were scared and ran our legs off all the way to Jahn's. Nervous about what happened, I told Mom a few days later and admitted we went to Jahn's. She said she told us not to go because it was too late and dangerous for us to be out. She was right; I was punished and I learned a lesson.

When Fran slept over, we usually shared the bed in the pull-out Castro convertible. We used to daringly think of song titles and put them in front of the phrase "under the sheets." Like: "Let the Good Times Roll" … under the sheets; "Shake, Rattle, and Roll" … under the sheets; "Don't Be Cruel" … under the sheets. Lorraine, who stammered a little since being hit by a car, must have been listening. Out of the darkness and quiet of the night came her voice saying, "T-T-T-Ten Little Indians." Fran and I laughed like crazy into our pillows, envisioning ten bouncing heads … under the sheets!

We were sitting on the stoop late one night talking, went up to go to bed, and everyone was asleep in the darkened house. With no lights, trying not to make any noise, quietly we changed, being careful not to bump into the Castro pullout. I walked around it to give Fran her pajamas; she avoided hitting it to give me my curlers. I asked her for my brush, and all of a sudden she started laughing hysterically out loud—the bed we had been walking around wasn't even opened! As we laughed, a few voices stirred, and George came ranting out of the nearby alcove in his underwear, mad as heck that Fran was there to see him that way. Fran and I just giggled ourselves to sleep.

After Fran moved, I started hanging around with Jeannette, who lived on 112th Street. Her mom made the best Italian sauce and pasta. Jeannette's older brother Bob was cool and kind of kept an eye on us. We hung around with him and his friends by Kavons, a little variety store on the south corner of Jerome and 114th Street, across the street from the Jerome movie. Sometimes the guys would play slap ball on the side of the movie wall, and the cops would pull up and tell them to stop or they would get "JD" (juvenile delinquent) cards. They weren't doing anything wrong or damaging, but they stopped. I loved it when the guys, in their black leather jackets and slicked-back hair, stood under the corner streetlight and sang in harmony. They did a great rendition of, "The Lion Sleeps Tonight." There were no fights, drinking, or cursing. We just hung around together talking. One night Jeannette told me her brother said we should never go to Smokey Park on 125th Street because there was a drug there called "mar-i-jew-ana." We never hung out at the park anyway, but we heard that tough kids used to meet there and have fights with garrison belts. It was about 1956, and it was the first time we ever heard about illegal drugs of any sort.

Across the street from the Jerome movie was a place where they made fresh, hot bagels. The workers were shirtless, usually in shorts with bandanas around their heads, as they sweated in front of the huge ovens. Many a Saturday night we ran or bicycled down 114th Street, following the aroma of the baking bagels, and sped home as quickly as we could with a hot dozen or more. Mom had the fresh coffee perking, the butter was out, and we all feasted on this wonderful delight.

Mom's kitchen was often a late-night gathering place. Mom liked to relax, read the papers, and have her coffee. She read every newspaper article from the first to last page. Many of our friends or dates would come over for coffee at the end of a night out and feel comfortable to sit around and talk about anything and everything. It was a very wise thing on Mom's part, since she could really get to know who our friends were. I enjoyed the rare occasions of quiet, coffee-for-two conversations with Mom and always felt free to share my feelings and concerns about life with her. She was a woman born before her time, very wise in her advice and steadfast in her beliefs.

Once we started high school, we girls were allowed to wear lipstick. We knew nothing about makeup. I wore bright red lipstick like Mom, and the boy next door made fun of me and called me "lips." As I got taller, he kept calling me "legs." I found out that pale pink lipsticks were "in" and switched to the softer shades. Some girls shaved their eyebrows off and made big arches with eyebrow pencils where they had shaven. Pancake makeup was used by a lot of girls, leaving them with white necks and pink or tan faces. I didn't like it and followed Mom's advice not to use that stuff because it clogged the pores and wasn't good for the skin. She was right—good old soap and water was the best! She didn't wear makeup but sometimes used cold cream at night. She avoided the sun because of the damage it caused and always had a beautiful complexion.

Sometimes we kids couldn't understand the punishments that were dealt us. One of us would do something wrong and have to stay in the house one day, while another of us would do the same thing and get grounded for a week. It just wasn't fair! Mom *always* had the same answer: "Each of you is unique. You're the same in many ways, but different in some ways, and as a result sometimes are treated a little differently. Each of you is unique." It took maturing and being a parent to see the wisdom and foresight in my mother's words.

Rock and Roll was a big hit in the 1950s. Chaperoned dances were held in most churches, and during the summer supervised dances were held outdoors at Victory Field in Forest Park, Queens. Teenagers came from all over Queens and Brooklyn to strut their stuff, dance their legs off, and scan the crowd, looking for someone good looking to date. If Dolores went, I was told to go to keep an eye on her. It was at Victory Field where Dolores met this great dancer from Woodhaven—Don McGuire. He saw Dolores and said to his friend, "I'll take the small one, you take the tall one." Another lifetime tale of love was evolving. Reenie wasn't a fan of dancing and would only go sometimes. If I went to a dance, Jeri, who also loved to dance, went with me and we were always told to watch each other—the old, "Keep an eye on your sister and report back." We always took a bus or train to get to any of these places where dances were held.

The Brooklyn Paramount Theatre was the scene of Rock and Roll live, and it was fantastic to go to a show, which I only did once. It was well worth the wait to go in and hear Alan Freed and Cousin Brucie introduce all those doo-wop entertainers whose music just stirred the soul. The place was jammed with teenagers, and my friend and I were seated so high up we were almost on the roof. I had a crush on the singer Jimmy Clanton, who sang "Just a Dream" and was so cute and known for his gorgeous light blue eyes. When he came on stage, I started screaming, "Look at his eyes! Look at his eyes!" We were so far up I could hardly see his head, no less his eyes, but I loved it!

The biggest hit of the '50s was Elvis (the Pelvis) Presley. When he was on the *Ed Sullivan Show*, the cameras only showed him from the waist up, due to his gyrations. My mom and Fran's mother were immediate fans and loved watching him perform. Fran and I loved his music and songs, which were great to dance to. He was good looking, but we were too young to understand our mothers', and most women's, behavior and reaction to him. I imagine most men didn't like Elvis because of his sexual appeal and how women went crazy over him.

It was 1956. Dad was 45, Mom was 42, George was 18, Dolores was 17, I was 14, Reenie was 13, Jeri was 11, Lorraine was 9, Raymond was 7, Eddie was 6, Dennis was 5, Robert was 3—and all ten of us welcomed our new brother, Thomas (Tommy), on December 30, 1956. (At year's end, he probably heard my parents talking about tax deductions!) He was over ten pounds, blonde-haired, blue-eyed, dimpled, and an absolute delight and quickly became the center of attention. Tommy was an armful; my cousin Fred Wolf and I, as his Godparents, can attest to this. I turned 15 and was so honored to be Godmother to my little brother. Ray, Eddie, Dennis, and Robert showed him the ropes. Robert, always happy and full of energy, doted on his new brother. Dennis, tender and soft-hearted by nature, took special care of him. Before you knew it, Tommy was right in there with all his brothers, learning to share toys and defend what was his. As the family kept growing, though, I often heard George complain that it wasn't fair. I guess he felt cheated out of things he couldn't have.

My brothers were all good, and I enjoyed taking care of them. On Saturday afternoons Mom would tell us girls, "Take the kids to the park, and don't come home until five o'clock." Pushing the carriage, Jeri, Reenie, and I made the little ones stop at each corner to look for cars before crossing, and at the park made sure they all stayed together and had fun. We'd push them on the swings, help them up the monkey bars, catch them at the slide, and made sure they didn't topple off the seesaw. Trips to the avenue were usually made with all the boys in tow. I'll never forget the time my little brothers and I were all on Liberty and Lefferts, across the street from Karp's Ice Cream Parlor. My brothers had to "go," and they decided to line up on the curb and have a "who-can-pee-the-farthest" contest. I could have died of mortification and wanted to run and hide. I gave all of them a lecture and a whack on the bottom and hurriedly took them home.

Christmastime was quite an event at our house. Mom would give me $2 and I would take each brother individually on the bus to Jamaica to do his Christmas shopping in Woolworth's. A 10¢ lipstick or 10¢ bracelet or pin for the girls and Mom, a few 5¢ packages of plastic soldiers or cowboys for the boys, a 5¢ coloring book, a 5¢ ball for the baby, a small shave cream for Dad, a 10¢ comb for George, and gifts were bought for everyone! At the end of the shopping spree, I usually treated whichever brother I took shopping to a 10¢ ice cream with syrup, using the money I got from babysitting or cleaning houses. When we got home, each brother would find his own "hiding place" for the presents he had bought after I assured him that he bought great gifts. It's amazing how you can stretch a dollar when you have to! Watching every penny, nickel, and dime is how you do it!

My father usually bought a Christmas tree on his way home from work, real close to Christmas to get the best price. One year Dad bought home two scrawny trees that must have been leftovers. The two trees were tied together to look like one, and the cord was tacked to the wall so they wouldn't fall over. Dad put the lights on the tree, and we all pitched in and decorated it, ending with the ever-sparkling tinsel. After the little ones went excitedly to bed on Christmas Eve, we all quietly put our wrapped presents under the tree. Mom and Dad then went down the basement and brought up their hidden "Santa" gifts—a new bike, carriage, doll, baseballs and bats, cowboy boots, Boy Scout camping gear, basketballs, clothes—and a whole lot of toys that jingled and jangled. Due to Dad's working so hard, gifts from Mr. Dunn from the church weren't necessary anymore. Scrawny or not, our Christmas tree was rooted in and surrounded by love, laughter, and joy!

On Christmas morning we all awoke really early to squeals of delight and surprise as the little ones saw that Santa had been there. Fresh coffee was perking as we opened our gifts and thanked each other with hugs and kisses. Wrapping paper was everywhere. Everyone was in the spirit, and we had to practically drag my brothers away from their new toys to eat and get ready for church. St. Bennies had a nine o'clock children's Mass that we all attended while still in grammar school. We bundled up in our holiday reds and greens to celebrate Christmas. The boys were in suits, ties, and polished shoes; the girls wore festive dresses, hats, gloves, and patent leather shoes. Mom and Dad very often attended Mass together on Christmas Eve. Sometimes, much to Mom's delight, Dad would say, "C'mon Sweetheart—this Christmas Eve we'll go to your church." And off they would go to St. Matthew's Lutheran church in Ozone Park, where Grandma Wolf and Aunt Julia worshipped. As some of us got older, we started attending Christmas Eve Mass. It was such a special occasion. The church was dimly lit. Angelic voices of the boy's choir filled the air as they walked down the aisle in their white robes trimmed in red, each holding a candle to light the way. Heartfelt, joyous tears were quietly shed, as the organ led us in song to celebrate the birth of Our Lord and Savior Jesus Christ.

One Christmas when I was a teenager, Dad gave me $150 and told me to buy some nice things for Mom. I bought a red dress (Mom's favorite color), a matching necklace, a red slip, a pretty robe, slippers, perfume, and a variety of "nighties," mostly red. They were always kissing and hugging and going away for romantic weekends together, so I figured they would be perfect for their "getaways." (Plus I was hearing more and more about *it*.) When Mom opened the alluring nightwear, the two of them were laughing and giving each other "the eye," and Mom was turning red while Daddy grinned from ear to ear. He probably grinned all the way to the reservation counter to schedule another weekend away!

Enveloped in the aroma of the roasting turkey or beef Mom was preparing, Christmas day was bursting with sounds of laughter as new games and toys were played with, new clothes, shoes, and jewelry tried on, and friends and family visited to share in the fun. When we were smaller and there were fewer of us, the Upton Family Christmas party was usually held at one of our aunt and uncle's house, where small gifts were exchanged due to the tough economy—a handkerchief, socks, gloves, a notepad, pen, tie, pin. As years passed and George and Vera's family grew, the Richmond Hill Uptons' was the place to celebrate. (Who wanted all of us at their house?) Aunts, uncles, and cousins came over. In order to have enough seats for everyone, we used to borrow chairs from Leahy Funeral Home on 118th Street. Mr. Leahy's generosity was fully appreciated, plus he probably figured—businesswise—that somewhere down the road it would pay off. My Cousin Jackie Upton's wife Gladys recently told me about the first time she came to our house for Christmas. As Santa (Dad) was distributing gifts, much to her surprise, Gladys's name was called. She was deeply touched that my parents gave her a gift, even though they didn't even know her yet. But that was Mom and Dad—always making sure no one was left out and that everyone felt welcome and part of the family.

We all looked forward to Aunt Julia and Uncle Herb Wolf's Christmas visit. They never had any children and always bought us gifts that were special. Uncle Herb had his own successful business, and Aunt Julia shopped in the prohibitively expensive small shops on Liberty Avenue—the kind where you stopped, looked in the window, and dreamed. One year they gave us girls beautiful Chinese-styled pajamas, and we danced around mimicking China dolls, which Dad caught on his eight-millimeter movie camera. The best was when they gave each of us girls a luxurious red-and-white striped nylon blouse that we all loved and wore to shreds.

I'm pretty sure Julia and Herb were our favorite aunt and uncle. They lived in the first-floor apartment of Grandma and Grandpa Wolf's house on 133rd Avenue and 114th Place in Ozone Park. When we visited, or they came over our house, Uncle Herb would enchant us with his Rumpelstiltskin skit from German folklore about a dwarf who spun flax into gold. Aunt Julia was nice to talk to, and she liked to fuss and primp with us girls. We'd usually visit Julia and Herb and Grandma and Grandpa at the same time. Treats were ours to have, but we never ate dinner there. We were a lot of mouths to feed! Once in a while Mom and Dad were invited for dinner alone to enjoy Grandma's scrumptious sauerbraten. I'm sure they savored the special dinner and quiet time with Mom's parents. (Naturally, as an ever-growing family, we didn't get too many invitations for dinner!)

Unfortunately, I have memories of some of my mother's family being against the fact that we kids were Catholic. If my sisters and I slept over Grandma's, she made sure we got to Sunday Mass on time. Uncle Bumpsy, who was divorced and living at Grandma's, would wake up complaining that he couldn't sleep and was annoyed that we had to go to Mass because we were Catholic. (He probably had a hangover.) Grandma, in her German accent, stated, "It vas rrright dat the cheeldren go to chuurch" She made sure our outfits were fit and proper, and off we went to Mass. Grandma and Grandpa loved my mother and her good-natured husband and were very accepting of how we kids were being raised.

Grandma Wolf had no idea that she spoke with an accent. Once, while discussing someone's heritage, Grandma asked if the person spoke English. I responded yes, but that the person had an accent similar to hers. *Well!* In a high-pitched tone, she said, "*Vat!* I haff no agsent! I speak *puuurr*fect English!" She spoke, wrote, and read English superbly but didn't know her German inflection was a presence. I quickly changed the subject—and quietly took my foot out of my mouth!

My mother's brother Pinky (Helmut) also married a Catholic, Aunt Charlotte. They had four children—Ronnie, Susan, Jimmy, and Maryellen, and lived in Alexandria, Virginia, since my uncle worked for the state department. Mom told us that as a child her brother Pinky was left-handed, which was thought to be a sign of mental problems then. In school, Pinky was forced to write with his right hand, which resulted in a slight stuttering of his speech. We have a lot of happy memories of visiting the "Virginia Wolfs," and they in turn came up and spent time in New York. My cousin Ronny came up once with a friend, and they wanted to go to Manhattan to see the "queers." My friend and I took them to a park in Greenwich Village, and Ronny said, "Where are they?" and I answered, "I don't know—I don't know what they look like." So much for metropolitanism!

Uncle Pinky converted to Catholicism like his wife. Sad to say, he was diagnosed with lung cancer, which ended his life at an early age. Mom was devastated and always said that the lung cancer was a result of his witnessing A-Bomb tests as part of his government job, before necessary protective precautions were taken. Naturally, we and all of Mom's family went to Virginia to attend Uncle Pinky's funeral. At the wake, when a Catholic priest came into the room to say prayers, Pinky's brothers Herb and Howie got up and angrily left the room, in total defiance of the Catholic service. It was a slap in the face to my grieving Aunt Charlotte and her children. The ecumenical words of my mother were recalled—"There is one God, called by different names, worshipped in varying ways. But there is one God." I thank God for Mom, a woman born before her time.

Elvira & George Upton – 1938

George, Jr. and Dolores Upton – May, 1943

Upton Kids: (l-r) Patty, George, Jeri, Dolores, Reenie – 1946

Rockaway Beach – 1948

(l-r) Patty, Reenie, Dolores, Jeri, George, Jr., George, Sr., Lorraine

Easter – 1953

(top-l) Reenie center row (l-r) baby Robert, Lorraine, Jeri, Patty, Raymond

(bottom) Eddie, Dennis

Staten Island Ferry – 1953

(top) Patty, Jeri, Reenie, George Upton, Sr.

(bottom) Raymond, Eddie

5 younger Upton boys: 1962
Tommy, Robert, Dennis, Eddie, Raymond

Tommy & Adrianne – 1962

Chapter 11

I remember when the doorbell rang and this real good-looking guy came bounding up the stairs, asking if Dolores was home. She wasn't, but when he said his name—Don McGuire—Mom asked him if his father was Jim McGuire who used to live on Marion Street in Brooklyn. Yep! Then she asked if his father drove an oil truck. Yep! His father grew up with my father, and when Don McGuire from Elderts Lane, Woodhaven, came looking for Dolores, he was in like flint! Don worked at the Brooklyn Navy Yard and later joined the NYPD. He and Dolores met at Victory Field, started dating, and before you know it were crazy about each other. Fran and I thought Don was an absolute hunk. Besides being good looking, Don was a great dancer and had a big green car. (I don't know what make it was. If it isn't a Volkswagen Beetle or a bus, I'm lost!)

Don and Dolores became engaged, and Reenie and I were thrilled to be asked to be in the bridal party. This wedding stuff was new to all of us. We all quickly learned about invitations, bridal showers, gown fittings, and photographers and rental cars. The day finally arrived! The bridal party wore elegant, light aqua blue gowns. Mom made sure my sisters wore pretty dresses and the boys were well suited. Dad looked so handsome in his black tux as he accompanied Mom, who wore a red silk dress with black sequin flowers on it. She was absolutely stunning. It was a dress that Mom loved and wore to a few more of our weddings. The photographer, Rubin, was a man who worked with my father at West Chemical.

On November 23, 1957, Dolores Upton and Donald McGuire were married at St. Benedict Joseph Labre Church. Dolores was beautiful in her white gown as she and her handsome groom started down a pathway of love. We all went to the reception at the Glenville Inn in Glendale. Don comes from a family of thirteen children, so needless to say it was a blast! The Upton and McGuire families that originated from Marion Street were together again! Because it was such a young bridal party, the DJ called for a lot of kissing events. I was 15 years old and felt embarrassed, and Reenie at 14 didn't like it either. Mom was watching like a hawk as all this kissing was taking place. Everyone had a good time, and Don and Dolores left on a honeymoon to New England. (After Dolores got married and moved out, the arguments over clothes stopped. So obviously she had been the culprit!)

Of course the wedding made me yearn for the day that I would fall in love and get married. Instead, when I turned 16, I got a job at Woolworth's in Jamaica as a cashier. It wasn't far from school, and I was paid 99¢ an hour! Using a cash register was a new experience. There was only cash then, no credit cards, and you had to total the sale, look up and ring in the taxes, and use your brain. When I worked at the candy and cookie counter, I was told that if I saw any roaches or rats, I had to catch them and get rid of them. Well, if I saw a roach or rat, they'd have to catch me because I'd be running! My girlfriend worked the hot dog and pizza counter, and she was told that on Mondays, since the store was closed Sunday, she had to wipe down the leftover already cooked hot dogs from Saturday and remove any mold from them and the leftover pizza slices. While working at the record counter, the song "Purple People Eater" was a big hit, and I played the song over and over and over again—while wearing a purple beanie with dangling wire antennas popping on my head. But I liked payday! I liked making money and didn't mind pitching in financially to help our large family. Sometimes I wished I could have participated in after-school activities, especially the plays at Dominican, but somebody had to catch those critters in Woolworth's!

After their wedding, Dolores and Don lived in a three-room apartment in Ozone Park. When Dolores became pregnant, we sisters were thrilled at the thought of becoming *aunts! Wow!* We loved going over their apartment and seeing what it was like to be married. We helped out where we could but actually ended up learning a lot from Dolores. She was a good cook and knew how to keep the apartment spic and span. On June 24, 1958, Donald McGuire Jr. was born. Between the McGuire and Upton families, did he have a lot of aunts and uncles and playmates—right down to his Uncle Tommy, who was now 1 ½ years old! Don Jr. fit right in with the rough and tumble ways of his uncles, and we new aunts loved to baby-sit.

George, a civil engineer, was now engaged to Margaret (Peggy) Joy, a New York City school teacher, and they were planning their wedding. I was still working at the five and dime and made it to senior year, in spite of being lousy in math. Algebra was Greek to me and totally baffled my mind. Just couldn't see how X equaled Y! One term I went to summer school for business arithmetic (idiot's math). It was the palest, most sunless summer I ever experienced. But I was now looking forward to graduation.

Everyone in the senior class was talking about and looking forward to religion class—"The Marriage Encyclical." We thought finally we'd get the scoop about *it,* but *it* never happened. It was more church history personified. The senior prom was the event we all looked forward to! In gym class, we wore ugly, green, baggy one-piece gym suits as the very prim and proper Mrs. Delaney concentrated on our dancing skills for the upcoming occasion. Since I was tall, I was always the boy! The senior prom was the biggie, and I went with Jack, who also escorted me to his senior prom at Bishop Loughlin. I wore the aqua blue bridesmaid gown from Dolores's wedding to both. After the prom, a bunch of us went to a nightclub, and then took the "Sunrise Cruise" on the Staten Island Ferry. In our gowns and tuxedos, we went by subway to Brooklyn for a wonderful breakfast that Pat K's mom prepared for us. We ended the day with a barbeque at Belmont Lake State Park. When I got home, exhausted, I told Mom and my brothers and sisters all about the great time I had.

Senior year was full of expectations and planning for the future. Passing Regent's exams was vital for graduating, and thankfully we were well prepared with an excellent secretarial education. On June 19, 1959, in our white caps and gowns, 318 voices sang our graduation theme song—"You'll Never Walk Alone." I felt like crying, especially when I looked out and saw my parents looking so happy and proud. I realized it was their love and constant sacrifices that brought me to this emotional day, and my heart was bursting with love and gratitude for them. Now I could go to work at a real job and help out more financially.

My parents had no idea of the demerits I accumulated during my four years at DC. For social reasons, I would have loved to have had a phone at home, but I was glad we didn't have one to receive demerit reports. Mom used to brag, "Both my daughters went to Dominican and neither of them ever got a demerit," as she was saying at a bridal shower one time. I finally told her that I hated to hear her lying, and that I had gotten thirty-three demerits—for goofy, stupid, innocent things, I assured her. My sisters laughed, not surprised at all, and once Mom picked her chin up from the floor, she joined in the laughter.

A few girls went on to college after graduation, some got engaged or married, but most of us got jobs as secretaries. A lot of girls got local jobs, but me—I wanted to work in New York City!

I was 17, went for an interview at a big financial company, got the job, and started right after graduation. Mom and Dad were excited for me, and I always sensed that by working in *the city* I was doing something that Mom in her heart had always wanted to do. Every day I took the subway to Columbus Circle and loved walking along Central Park South to Madison Avenue and 59th Street. Those were times when working in Manhattan called for class and elegance. Women wore skirts (you remember—those things where your legs hung out), high heels, and gloves. Now they schlep around in sneakers and jeans.

My job was as secretary for an assistant Vice President (don't be impressed—the entire floor I worked on was filled with assistant VPs). I loved midtown! A whole new world opened in front of me. My naiveté showed when I ate in restaurants where I didn't even understand the menus, and my date would order for me. There was so much silverware in front of me I thought I was sharing my dinner with someone else. Broadway shows were a whole new experience. A date once took me to an off-off-Broadway show. It was in someone's apartment, and we sat in a circle of chairs as the actors darted in and out of the inner circle to perform. We applauded by clapping our index fingers, so as not to disturb the neighbors. It was one of many new experiences that came with working in the city, and I loved every minute of it.

Since I was working in Manhattan, I needed a new winter coat, so Mom and I went shopping in Goodwin's in Jamaica. Mom always had a "buy a bigger size—you'll grow into it" attitude about clothing. I found a coat I liked, and with Mom's guidance, bought it in size 16! I'm still a 10, and in my life never wore a 16! I may have invented the baggy look! I'm glad I never grew into it! As with all the clothing in the family, it got passed down to the next sister in line. Since it was so big, Reenie and Jeri could have worn it together! I replaced it with a very simple, elegant white coat in my size.

I loved payday, and every Friday I bought Mom a bouquet of flowers at the train station. I had no qualms about giving a portion of my pay to Mom and Dad, knowing it would help with household expenses. I met some very nice people at work, and this girl Marlene and I hit it off right away. I once showed her the new baby-toed shoes I bought on sale, and she said they were on sale because they were out of style. Style? What's that? When she came for dinner at my house things were always jumping. She was an only child and lived in a nice, very quiet house in Queens. She had a lovely, spacious bedroom, and the first time I slept over her house her mother handed me some towels and said, "Pat, these are yours to use." And the towels were D-R-Y!!!

Chapter 12

As George and Peggy's wedding day neared, a bachelor party was held for George at a local bar. George was never a drinker, but quite a few of his college friends were. The purpose of a bachelor party (which I never did understand) was to get the groom soused. Well, they did a good job. It was getting late, and Mom was anxiously awaiting the return of George and Dad from the bachelor party when we heard noise and laughter at the bottom of the stairs. Dad and his friend John Robertson were laughing their heads off as they were trying to carry George's limp body up the stairs. I guess in my father's eyes his son had attained manhood. He was sick as a dog, and Mom was so upset at my father for laughing. She kept saying, "My baby—my poor baby." I was laughing too as they finally got him in the house and laid him on his bed, out like a light. Mom got a pail and put it next to George's bed, and said since I thought it was so funny, I had to take charge of the pail and make sure George didn't miss it. It wasn't any fun doing "pail patrol," and I stopped laughing pretty quickly. Believe me, George's bachelor party caused quite an "upheaval" in the house that night!

George Upton Jr. and Margaret Joy were married August 22, 1959, in Our Lady of Perpetual Help church in Richmond Hill. Jeri, then 14, tall and slim, was in the bridal party, and the reception was held at Leonard's of Great Neck. The newlyweds spent their wedding night at the International Hotel at Kennedy Airport, and when they got back from their honeymoon, George showed everyone the photos of airplanes he had taken from their room that night. George was always an airplane enthusiast and ended up working as a civil engineer for Pan American. But my father kept razzing George that he couldn't believe *his son* spent his wedding night taking pictures of planes!

Even though I loved my job, after a few months I was getting antsy and wanted more of a challenge. I went on one interview at a brokerage house downtown Manhattan in the financial district. The building was ancient, the old elevators were run by uniformed operators who opened and closed the creaky elevator gate at each floor, and the streets were old, narrow, and crowded. *Nah*—not for me. On my second interview—in midtown—I got a secretarial position on Park Avenue and 51st Street at a prestigious investment counseling company. Across the street was the Waldorf Astoria, where John Kennedy stayed while in New York. Whenever he was in town, everyone crammed by the windows of the twenty-second floor to catch a glimpse of him. St. Patrick's Cathedral, Saks Fifth Avenue, and Rockefeller Center were right up the street, along with some great clothing stores.

Mom and Dad were so happy and excited when I told them of my new job and the big increase in pay. I felt proud and pleased to know I could contribute more money to the family. There was one difference though—*I only got paid once a month!* I still bought Mom flowers every Friday, and each payday I bought something special for one of my brothers or sisters, usually an outfit of some sort, or we'd go shopping for new shoes. Between buying new clothes for myself, going out dancing with friends, and taking a lot of taxis, my money usually petered out the week before payday. Mom was there for a temporary bailout!

It was 1959. I was graduated and working in New York City, Dolores and Don were expecting their second child, George and Peg were married, and Mom and Dad continued taking their romantic bus trips together, very often to New England, Niagara Falls, Atlantic City, Quebec, or Montreal. They were always affectionate and loving and through the years looked forward to their relaxing getaways. Mom had to be as tired from her never-ending care of us kids as Dad was from working two full-time jobs. The older ones of us were certainly responsible enough to watch our siblings so they could cherish their time together with peace of mind.

On November 28, 1959, my girlfriend I went to the "18 and over" dance held at St. Fortunatas church on Linden Boulevard, Brooklyn. (I don't know how I got in—I was only 17.) My friend and I promised each other we'd be sure to go home together. The music was good, my blonde hair was in a long ponytail, and I was wearing a red sweater. (Mom always said guys loved red!) There was a sailor in his winter blues who kept asking me to dance. His name was Bill. He was good looking and a real good dancer and was home on his first leave after boot camp. He asked if he could drive me home, and I said no. Then my girlfriend told me that she was going home with a guy she met, and I sure didn't want to walk to the bus stop alone. When Bill asked me to dance again, I said maybe I would take that ride home—but I'd sit in the backseat to play it safe. He said, "Fine, you can sit on the roof if you want to." He drove me straight home and asked for my phone number, but we still didn't have one. He said he'd write from Virginia, where he was stationed, so he could take me out when he came home for the weekend. I said, "Fine, thanks for the ride," and waited for him to come around and open the car door for me. Soooo … this was the sarcastic beginning of my relationship with Bill Stamm—the man I would end up marrying.

My girlfriends and I used to go different places to dance and meet guys. We started going to Rockaway to this place called "The Last Stop" on Broad Channel Drive and 116th Street. Some of my girlfriends liked to drink beer, but I ordered a screwdriver and nursed it all night because I just wanted to dance. Mom always wanted to know where I was going and who I was going with. She swore she was going to show up to check it out, no matter where I went, and I didn't doubt she would. Once she asked me where I was going, and I said, "Some Place Else." She thought I was wising off, but I explained that it was a dance place in Freeport. She said, "Don't be surprised if I show up there." Even though we didn't have a car and she would have to take two buses to get there, knowing Mom, I was always aware of the possibility of her showing up!

There really was no reason for Mom's concern, because I was not a drinker, loved to dance, and was very aloof when it came to the opposite sex. I was probably a big disappointment to a lot of dates, but my message was loud and clear—*no!* I dated a guy who lived on First Avenue in Manhattan who took two buses and a train to get to my house. His persistent advances were turned down, and he gave up after two more long, fruitless trips. Guess he got the message—*no!* I think Mom had the normal motherly concerns about daughters dating. If any of the boys my sisters and I dated had a car, Mom and Dad would send my brothers outside to write down the license plate number, and then they had to leave their full name, address, and phone number before we could leave on a date. Have a nice time!

I was meeting and dating different guys, including Bill Stamm, when he came home on weekends. I'd go with a date to the movies on Friday night, go out to dinner and dancing with another on Saturday night, and maybe go to a Yankee game with someone else on Sunday afternoon. My father was going crazy having so many different guys coming to date his daughters and couldn't remember their names. One guy I dated, a lefty, gave my left-handed brother Eddie his baseball glove from Brooklyn Tech

High School. Getting to me through my lovable brothers didn't work, but Eddie still remembers. Mom and Dad both liked Bill. Like Don McGuire with the Irish name, Stamm had it made with his German name. Grandma Wolf always said his name was probably "Von Shtamm" at one time. I only knew him a couple of weeks when I saw Bill at Christmas Eve Mass, shivering in the back of the church in his navy blues. Afterward we walked home, and he gave me a lovely cross on a chain for Christmas. He also bought some toys for my younger brothers. Boy, was he trying to make points! I had already received Christmas gifts from two other dates (see, young ladies out there, it pays to say *no!*). Oh, by the way, when I was dating these different gentlemen, Mom was pregnant and expecting a baby in June! It didn't faze me in the least—Mom was always pregnant. I never gave it a thought that my dates might be surprised, intimidated, or taken aback.

Don and Dolores's second child, Doreen, was born in 1959 and greeted her blonde-haired, blue-eyed sister Denise a year and a half later. The McGuire family moved into the large apartment over Grandma and Grandpa Wolf's candy store on Rockaway Boulevard. I loved to babysit for them, and when the kids were toddlers we would "have a parade." With spoons to bang the pots and pans in hand and pot lids on our heads, we paraded and marched around the apartment and had a grand old time. The woman now renting the candy store downstairs said she heard us and the ceiling lights would shake. My grandparents still owned the building but no longer ran the candy store, because Grandpa was sick. He had heart trouble, and his body kept filling with fluids. He wouldn't go to a hospital because he thought hospitals were a place to die. Mom sent Dr. Ralph over to see him, much to Julia and Herb's disapproval, because Dr. Ralph was Jewish! (How small-minded and ridiculous!) Grandpa enjoyed Dr. Ralph.

They were from the same generation of immigrants and talked a lot about the "old country" and things of the past. He made house calls a few times a week, but Grandpa was not doing well.

Bill Stamm had shore duty in Portsmouth, Virginia, and would come home weekends however he could. He once caught a flight on a two-seated plane and flew into Floyd Bennet Field in Brooklyn. From there he hitched a ride on a motorcycle and looked a little green by the time he got to my house. He didn't have a car, so most of the time we walked to wherever, usually holding hands. We're still hand-holders to this day. On the way home from the RKO Keith's one night, on our second or third date, it started raining, so we quickly ducked into a store doorway to stay dry. All of a sudden his arms were around me, and this audacious fellow was kissing me. I was starting to like him, but how dare he! Sometimes he borrowed his father's car to take me on a date. One time he was driving north on Woodhaven Boulevard and was signaling to make a left turn into Forest Park, where I heard "Lover's Lane" was. I quietly said, "If you're going in there to park—I don't park!" He then made the slowest, longest, most silent U-turn on record and finally pulled over on a well-lit corner and said, "Is this bright enough?" He just kept saying he had never met anyone like me.

We once stopped over his house, and I met his parents and got the definite impression he had never brought a girl home before. Bill was the fourth of five children, Barbara, Joan, John, Bill, and Marilyn. Bill's brother was getting married in February, and he asked me to go with him. I bought a new dress but wasn't quite sure how tall Bill was or what shoes to wear—flats, high heels, or medium heels. Since I was now 5'9", when he came to the door, I greeted him with medium heels on and changed into the spiked ones. Bill is 6 foot 1. *Phew!* During the reception we danced all night and Bill took me from table to table and introduced me to every aunt, uncle, cousin, and friend who was there. (He missed the waiters.) I had seen a picture of him before he went into the navy, and he had a sleazy mustache, greased-back hair, and looked like a hood. I never would have danced with him or dated him, for sure. The sailor I met was clean-cut and shaven and treated me like gold. I guess he never did meet anyone like me before. After a few months of dating, Bill bought me a beautiful pearl necklace that I still have, still wear, and will always treasure.

CHAPTER 13

Meanwhile, Grandpa Wolf was not doing well and was eventually hospitalized. In early March 1960, he passed away. Mom was devastated, and there was great concern for her health, especially since she was six months pregnant. She was inconsolable, but Dad was with her, wrapping her in his arms and his love, trying to shield her from the pain of loss she was feeling. But God is good, and before you knew it, they were sharing in the joy and elation of having their twelfth child. Brown-eyed with brown hair, beautiful Adrianne was born June 19, 1960, much to the delight of all of us (I think!). After all these years, a new sister to love! Six boys and six girls—perfect! Since George was born first and Adrianne last, they were the only ones who did not suffer from middle child syndrome! On the day she was born, baby Adrianne already had a niece and a nephew—Don Jr. and Doreen—and became an aunt for the third time in October 1960 when blonde-haired, blue-eyed Stephen Upton, George and Peggy's first child, was born. Under the circumstances, the formal title of aunt was dropped and they were all just playmates and friends.

Being the twelfth child, some of my brothers and sisters say Adrianne was spoiled. I never thought so. Things had certainly improved financially through the years, but I never thought she was treated differently or doted upon as a child. She wasn't fluffed up in lace and silk, had a buster brown haircut like we all had had, and wore hand-me-down striped polo shirts from her brothers. Of course, as she grew up she did live a different lifestyle, because times changed and improved financially. Having five brothers right before her gave Adrianne some pretty protective security.

She was a good baby, quiet by nature, and a pleasure to take care of. I'm sure Mom enjoyed having a little girl after all those years. From the day she was born, Adrianne looked like Mom. Once when I took her to a friend's house, my friend opened the door, saw Adrianne, and said, "Well, come in Mrs. Upton."

Everyone was growing older now, and the different personalities were evolving as each unique person emerged from within. Some of us were opinionated and outspoken, while others were quieter and just rolled with the flow. I was finding my niche and loved to spend time with Dolores, always asking her advice about boys and dating. Reenie was a quiet girl, kept to herself a lot, and excelled as she approached her last year at Bishop McDonnel High School. Not always a happy camper, she often voiced a complaint about having so many siblings. Jeri was outgoing, loved to dance and socialize, always pitched in and helped, and was doing well at Our Lady of Wisdom Academy. Lorraine, friendly but on the quiet side, always having fun with her friend Carol, had switched from OLWA to Richmond Hill High School. Raymond, Eddie, Dennis, and Robert were all in St. Bennies, each learning and growing into fine young gentlemen. They were always busy with the neighborhood kids playing games, riding bikes, pulling wagons, and of course playing stickball or organized baseball—*always* sticking together, as taught. All my younger brothers were on St. Bennie's baseball teams, and later participated in all the supervised activities at the Boy's Club, which opened on Atlantic Avenue and 110th Street. One of my favorite pictures is of my younger brothers—Ray, Eddie, Dennis, Robert, and Tommy—all lined up in front of the house in their SBJL baseball uniforms. They were so cute and happy, you just want to hug each of them!

As the boys got older, they used to keep all their baseball bats in a metal bin at the bottom of the stairs, convenient for easy grabbing on the way to a game. Late one night, when everyone was already in bed, Spooky, an excellent watchdog, started barking and growling like crazy by the rear window. Someone was in the yard! All my brothers ran downstairs in their underwear, each grabbing a bat on the way out. They chased the guy down, and the police came and took him away. Poor fellow—he had *no* idea he was trying to break into the wrong house!

Raymond was and still is a very gentle, warm-hearted person, always available to pitch in and help. To this day he kids Eddie that he was blamed and got in trouble for some of Eddie's shenanigans. Eddie had a way of pulling off a stunt and looking as innocent as an altar boy. If Grandma was visiting or babysitting, she would often sit quietly on the couch in deep contemplation while massaging her fingers. Eddie, sitting among his brothers playing, would let out an ear-piercing shriek from the side of his mouth—"rrreeee*eeeekk*"—and Grandma would jump sky high and ask who did it. Eddie would point a finger, and his angelic look usually got him off the hook. So Raymond was right—because of his innocence he took a few undeserved raps. Eddie and I are alike in many mischievous ways. I've seen him, straight faced and serious, tell many a tall tale to a group of people, waiting for their shocked reaction. When he looks my way, I simply say, "You can't snow the snowman."

In May 1961, Mom and Dad and all twelve of us gathered on the steps of St. Bennies to have a family picture taken. The picture appeared on the front page of the newspaper announcing that the *Long Island Press* had chosen George Upton as its "Long Island Father of the Year," and Mom and Dad were celebrating their twenty-fifth wedding anniversary. We all have this picture on display in our homes. All the boys from George on down looked so handsome and happy in their suits, one cuter than the other.

Dolores, Lorraine, Reenie, Jeri, and I were right above them, and Adrianne—eleven months—was held in her Daddy's arms.

Through the years on 114th Street, Mom and Dad made a lot of improvements on the house. New shingles covered the house with green upstairs and grey on the bottom. The original stoop was replaced with a new brick one, with an extended platform that turned right where new steps were added, and all was trimmed with a black wrought-iron railing. At the bottom was Mom's garden, which she hand-bordered with bricks and tended to all the time. The driveway was dirt down the middle, with a cement walkway on each side. With Robert's help, Mom and Raymond—on their hands and knees—cemented and installed bricks over the dirt, and it really looked nice. All of these changes added a whole new dimension to the Upton house, which stood out among the rest. Don McGuire and his friend Richie turned the cellar into a finished basement. They wood paneled all the walls, painted the lolly columns, put in recessed lighting, and installed a drop ceiling and a new vinyl floor. It was incredible! The family Christmas party and many occasions were celebrated thereafter in the newly finished basement.

It was down in the new basement that a friend showed me how to do a new dance called the "slop." To the tune of "Kansas City" by Wilbert Harris I eventually loosened up and got the hang of it. My brothers played nok-hockey and those hand-manipulated football games down there. A room in the center of the basement was filled with board games, books, and all sorts of things to keep everyone busy. All prom gowns, uniforms, and whatever were stored there for safe keeping. It was used for storing cases of canned goods, coffee, and other items that Mom bought in bulk when they were on sale. As a teenager, my brother Eddie and his friends formed a band and set up their equipment down the basement. I loved sitting on the basement steps listening and watching as Eddie, guitar in hand, belted out, "I Can't Get No Satisfaction." He loved the Rolling Stones and a lot of other groups, but the Beatles most of all. Years later I called him the night John Lennon was killed, knowing he would be in deep mourning for one of his idols.

A place that a lot of teenagers—of dating and driving age—went to was White Castle, located at the intersection of Liberty Avenue and Rockaway Boulevard, near Crossbay Boulevard. You'd pull your car into a parking spot, roll down the window, and the uniformed waitress (not on roller skates) walked over and took your order. She'd return with a tray filled with White Castle hamburgers and hang it on your window. The burgers were small, steam-cooked, topped with steamed onions, and cost about 12¢. You couldn't eat enough; they tasted so good! We called them "belly bombs," because as good as they tasted, they just laid in your stomach ready to burst. Guys would arrive by the car full, check out the chicks, and see who was driving what kind of souped-up set of wheels. Some of the guys met later at night to compete in drag races on Crossbay Boulevard to see whose car was the fastest. Pizza City and the Bow Wow were also popular eateries that drew a crowd of dragsters. New competition, Wetson Hamburgers, opened on Crossbay and Rockaway Boulevard.

One day at work an announcement was made that the president of the company had gone fishing and caught some salmon. An invitation was extended to all the investment counselors, secretaries, and their families to join in the feast. I was so proud when Mom and Dad and my younger brothers, all nicely dressed and on their best behavior, came and could see where I worked. It was a Friday evening, and Bill Stamm showed up in uniform. I introduced my family and Bill to everyone I worked with and showed them the desk I worked at, and then we all partook of the wonderful food that was prepared for us. Mom and Dad totally enjoyed the whole event and seeing where their daughter worked on Park Avenue, and I was bursting with pride and joy at the opportunity for them to do so. It was their priority of education and hard work that got me there.

Chapter 14

Bill and I started going steady, wrote to each other all the time, and most weekends he came home on leave. I had no idea that my Uncle Herb, who had a machine shop on Canal Street, took Bill to a jeweler he knew to make sure he got a good buy on an engagement ring. We were crazy about each other, and when he asked me to marry him I said yes—but he knew he had to first get my father's permission. Mom was cooking Sunday dinner with a smirk on her face, knowing Dad—with his sense of humor—would give Bill a hard time. Dad knew why Bill was nervously sitting silent and asked him to help him move some stuff down the basement. Well, they were down there forever, and I was nervous thinking my father was really giving him the third degree. They finally came upstairs, my father laughing his head off, and Bill laughing and looking relieved. He said he was getting tired of moving stuff around and figured he better ask my Dad's permission before they rearranged the whole basement! So now there was another wedding to plan!

Bill was transferred to the USS *Saratoga*, an aircraft carrier stationed in Portsmouth and leaving for a six-month Mediterranean cruise. We wrote to each other all the time. While he was away, I spent a lot of time with friends bowling at Americana Lanes. When looking at reception halls, I saw and liked a new place that was still under construction—the Huntington Townhouse. Ours would be one of the first weddings held there. I showed my parents the brochure and prices, and they said there was no problem. The date was set for May 1963. (Of course I selfishly never gave thought to how my family and friends—who all lived in the city—would get out there!) I wanted all of my sisters to be in my bridal party and told them I would pay for their gowns. I chose Dolores as my maid of honor. She was my mentor, and we had grown very close and became good friends and confidantes. Adrianne, who was 2, was too small to even be a flower girl.

Now that we were engaged, it was time for the formality of our parents to meet each other. My parents invited Bill's parents—John and Margaret Stamm—for dinner. Mom was actually rather shy when it came to social necessities such as these. After all the kids were fed, Mom and Dad sat down and had dinner with Bill's parents. They talked and had coffee and cake, and my sisters and I did the dishes. Then my parents were invited to Bill's house—not for dinner, but a social evening. When asked what they'd like to drink, Dad said a high-ball and Mom said nothing. Bill's Mom said, "Vera, I'll make you something I think you'll like—a Manhattan." Mom didn't know how to drink, and Dad told her to sip it slowly. Instead she whapped it down in one gulp like a kid taking medicine; *yuck*—do it fast and get it over with! Bill's mom no sooner sat down, saw Mom's empty glass and said, "Vera, would you like another?" Mom said yes, as my father was shaking his head trying to tell her to sip it and drink it slow. All in all, Mom drank five Manhattans in a row, each one going down like a shot. In walked Bill's brother and his friends drinking beer, and they were arguing with each other about something. Well, within two minutes Vera was smack dab in the middle of them giving her opinion about what they were loudly discussing. Mom was holding up okay, and when we took her home I'm sure she slept like a baby.

Bill returned home from the Mediterranean cruise with tons of gifts he bought for me—things he bought in Lebanon, Italy, and France and everywhere else he went. My mother's mouth fell to the floor when I opened one of the gifts—a r-e-a-l French bikini! She said, "Bill, what were you thinking when you bought that?" Thankfully he didn't answer. I tried it on and showed her, and she said—hesitantly—"Well, it really does look good on you." *Phew!* I loved it and wore it 'til it fell apart.

Since Bill enlisted in the navy just before his 18th birthday in September 1959, he was on "the Kiddy Cruise," which meant serving three years instead of four. Nearing the end of his three-year commitment, he was looking forward to getting out of the service when it was discovered that Russian ships were supplying Cuba, ninety miles off Florida, with nuclear missiles. In October I remember seeing and hearing the bone-chilling message that was aired on TV by a very somber President John Kennedy, saying the United States was sending our military ships and planes to confront the Russian ships. Fear of a nuclear World War III loomed throughout America. All military personnel serving then were extended a year, and all military reserves and national guardsmen were called to active duty, due to the Cuban Missile Crisis. I was petrified. Bill came home that weekend and said his ship was being sent to stop the Russians, and it didn't look good. He said, "Let's get married next weekend!" I was 20 years old, absolutely crazy about Bill, didn't want to die a virgin without finding out about *it,* and I said *yes!*

In a week's time, our wedding was planned. The Patio Club, a catering hall on Atlantic Avenue near city line, was available since another couple had to cancel because the groom was called to active duty. All the wedding invitations to family and friends were extended by phone. I hadn't yet gotten my gown or my sisters' gowns, so the bridal party was shortened to the maid of honor. George drove me to try on bridal gowns of friends who offered them, but nothing seemed right. When I got home tired and frustrated, hanging from the chandelier was the most simple, beautiful, elegant wedding gown I had ever seen. It belonged to Dolores's neighbor and fit like it was made for me. Dolores, my maid of honor, borrowed a red velvet dress for the occasion, so all was falling into place. I even had a bridal shower! It was not totally a surprise, though. I walked into Bill's house, and there on the enclosed front porch was my friend, Madeline V, peeking out the opposite side windows looking for me. I said, "Madeline, what are you doing here?" Well, was *she* surprised! And so was I to see so many people there at such short notice with beautiful gifts to start Bill and me off in our life together.

The girls at work had a luncheon for me and gave me a beautiful gift. Knowing there was a lot to do in a short time, after work I went to Plymouth Shop up the corner on Fifth Avenue and bought a variety of nightgowns. A girl's gotta do what she's gotta do! When Bill came home for the wedding, we went to the rectory for our prenuptial talk with the priest. He said I, as a wife, was to be very gentle when touching my husband. (Typical male thing!) He also told the both of us that we should never lock the bathroom door—it was a sign of mistrust. Sooooo … obviously, between the priest's talk and the nightgowns I bought, we were all set for marriage!

A few days before the wedding, Mom brought me into the kitchen for a private talk. Mom said she was going to tell me something that I was *not* to repeat to anyone. (Being the tallest girl, I figured she was finally going to tell me I was adopted!) Instead, in a low whisper, she proceeded to tell me that when she was pregnant with me, she had tuberculosis. I was relieved, and responded that I knew she had had TB. Her voice went up ten levels, and she said, *"Who told you?"* I didn't know who told me. It was just something I knew, and she made me promise not to tell anyone else. In those days, everything was a "secret." Sicknesses and diseases were treated like crimes and were hidden.

Our wedding day, November 3, 1962, was a bitter cold, wind-driven, rainy day. The photographer, Rubin, Dad's friend from work, was there snapping pictures, as Mom and Dad were getting everyone fed, dressed, and ready. Bill's brother, John, the best man, drove the rented Cadillac. Dolores was beaming in her red velvet dress. When the organ started playing I realized I forgot my bouquet of flowers! Don drove home to get them, while Bill's family was muttering, "She forgot her flowers—she'll fit right in the family!" As Daddy, so handsome in his tuxedo, walked me down the aisle, he said I looked beautiful and he loved me. (He also fit in a few I-won't-repeat wisecracks.) Mom looked beautiful in her favorite red silk dress with the black sequined floral design, as she and Dad sat with my brothers and sisters. Adrianne, then 2, was nestled in Daddy's arms.

The wedding reception was not until five o'clock, so Bill and I took Dolores and John for breakfast at the Sheraton Hotel at LaGuardia Airport. I ended up forgetting my flowers three times that day—at church, the Sheraton, and the photographer's studio, where a ton of pictures were taken. The reception at the Patio Club was perfect—great band, good food, and a lot of family and friends. There were no champagne toasts then—everyone toasted with a Manhattan. (Guests had the choice of a bottle of rye or scotch at their table in those days, and the average wedding gift was $25.) Being a dancing family, my brothers, Ray, Eddie, Dennis, Robert, and Tommy, were courteously asking different ladies to dance—the bride included. My sisters were on the dance floor with cousins. Mom and Dad danced romantically, as they often did in our living room. Adrianne was being babysat at the home of the Joys, Peggy's parents, so she missed seeing Eddie, 12, catch the garter and put it on the leg of the girl who caught the bouquet. "Daddy's Little Girl" in high heels was taller than him when we danced to that special song.

We spent the night near Kennedy Airport and took a flight Sunday for a weeklong honeymoon in glorious, balmy, tropical, palm-shaded—Portsmouth, Virginia. We rented an efficiency apartment and had a very romantic week together. Of course I finally learned about *it*. *It* sure was better than learning it from the nuns! When the week was up, after a very difficult and tearful good-bye on both our parts, I came back from our honeymoon alone. Dad and George met me at the airport and told me Mom was in the hospital with unclarified "woman" problems. We went immediately to see her. As usual, there was never a word of complaint from Mom, who looked very tired but assured me she was fine. (Through the years, Mom had a few miscarriages, which she explained as God's way of stopping something that wasn't growing right.)

After Mom got home and things settled down, Dolores drove me around to look at apartments. Mom wisely advised all of us when we got married not to move too close to either family; start your life together without interference. We found a nice three-room ground-floor apartment in a little apartment house on Myrtle Avenue and 115th Street. Bill came home by surprise one Friday night and told me not to tell his mom. (I may be blonde, but I'm not stupid!) We had a lot of stuff from the bridal shower—dishes, towels, sheets, blankets, coffee pot, etc.—but we didn't have a stick of furniture. We found a great store on Jamaica Avenue—General Furniture Warehouse—and furnished the entire apartment at discounted prices. We spread the word about this furniture warehouse, and a lot of our family and friends bought furniture there.

The Cuban Missile Crisis ended, the Russians backed off, and all military extensions of duty were canceled. By mid-December Bill was out of the navy and home for Christmas, and we had the biggest, most sparsely decorated Christmas tree in town to fill our then spacious, empty living room. It didn't matter—we were together. I was still working in the city, and Bill got a job in printing as a lithographer, which he was trained for. We bought a new Rambler, making sure whatever car we bought was big enough to fit Mom, Dad, and the kids for trips to amusement parks, beaches, and whatever outings we took.

With our rush of a wedding due to the Cuban Missile Crisis, I never gave thought to the fact that people would think I was pregnant when we got married. Impossible! It never entered my mind, until a year later on our anniversary my mother-in-law said, "Everybody in work can't believe it. A year already and no baby." Actually, as time went on, I was starting to wonder why I wasn't pregnant, especially since Bill and I both wanted to have a lot of kids.

When we got married I did not know how to cook. Without a list and instructions from Mom, food shopping was a whole new experience. By habit, I bought everything in bulk. We had enough mustard, ketchup, soup, pasta, bread, toilet tissue, and soap to take care of an army. We invited a couple for dinner, and a friend showed me how to make veal parmesan, suggesting I make spaghetti with it. When I looked into the box of spaghetti, I knew a pound wouldn't be enough—so I made four pounds! I had enough starchy water to wallpaper the whole apartment! One Saturday afternoon, while I was making supper the doorbell rang. I answered the door with tears in my eyes, and Dolores backed away and asked if Bill and I were having a fight. I whimpered,

"No, the cheese keeps coming out of the manicotti." Gratefully Dolores—aka Mary Poppins—came to the rescue!

Bill and I always met after work at the Eighth Avenue subway station in Kew Gardens, where we took the Lefferts Boulevard bus home. The bus was always jammed with riders, and one time I was sitting on the long side seat near the back, and Bill was standing in front of me, hanging on to the overhead strap. I looked up and could have died—his fly was open! With so many people around, I didn't want him to have to lean down as I told him, then quickly zip up and be embarrassed. So, having six brothers and being very adept with this situation, I nonchalantly reached forward to quickly close his fly. But in those days, all good secretaries wore gloves—and my white glove got caught in his zipper! Bill was mortified, I could have died, and everyone on the bus was astonished and laughing hysterically. I tried to get the glove loose, but instead Bill told me to take my hand out of it—and we got off the next stop, with my white glove dangling from Bill's zipper. So much for saving him embarrassment! As honking cars passed by at the sight of us, the glove was finally removed, and we walked home arm in arm. I was so thankful that Bill was a patient man, and we were newlyweds who were crazy about each other. Maybe it was because of things like that that my brothers and sisters, lovingly and with humor, started calling my husband "Poor Bill"—and still do to this day!

We were married a short time when Mom sent the insurance man over to sell us life insurance. Life insurance? We were young and healthy—we were not going to die! Mom, in her wisdom, explained the importance of life insurance, and the advantage of buying it at a young age. She spoke from experience, because Dad never had life insurance. Mom used to bug him about getting insurance, and when he finally applied he was turned down because he had high blood pressure. To offset this financial vacancy, Mom always invested their spare money in stocks and bonds and real estate. Very wise and fruitful choices were made.

With Dad working two full-time jobs and Mom saving wisely and spending carefully, things became easier financially for them. Mom and Dad took the boys on trips to dude ranches, amusement parks, and quite a few vacations to Canada and Florida. If Adrianne was too small to go, usually Dolores and Don or Bill and I babysat and enjoyed her thoroughly. Bus trips to Atlantic City, *before* the gambling casinos were there, became quite common. The boardwalk was beautiful as you walked past inviting shops and restaurants, the white sandy beach stretching endlessly on the shore. The long piers were filled with all sorts of amusement rides. I'm sure my younger brothers had a blast on the rides and in the ocean and pool. Mom and Dad often went to Atlantic City alone and continued their romantic getaways to Montreal, Quebec, and Niagara Falls to enjoy special time together.

The family was growing up! Reenie attended St. Joseph's School of Nursing in Yonkers and lived there; Jeri went on scholarship and resided at Queens General Hospital School of Nursing; Lorraine went to Richmond Hill High School and then went to work at Nestles Co. Raymond graduated from Richmond Hill High School and joined the New York City Police Department as a police cadet at age 17. Eddie attended Brooklyn Tech High School and had always wanted to go to the U.S. Air Force Academy to fulfill his love of aeronautics. He had the necessary endorsement from Judge Conroy, who lived on our street, but unfortunately had a tobogganing accident and seriously injured his leg. Thank goodness for the foresight of Dr. Ralph's son, also a doctor, who looked deeper into the injury and diagnosed osteomylitis, a very debilitating bone infection if not found and treated. It saved

Eddie a lot of painful consequences but unfortunately made him ineligible to attend the USAFA. He continued his studies at NY School of Aeronautics near LaGuardia Airport and other aeronautic institutions through the years. Dennis went to NY School of Printing in Manhattan, and Robert attended Bishop Loughlin High School in Brooklyn. Tommy was still in St. Bennies, and Adrianne was home with Mom, which I have a feeling they both enjoyed.

On May 2, 1964, beautiful, slender Jeri married Daniel Kline, who worked at the New York City department of sanitation in Queens. Adrianne, who was almost 4, was at the reception with all of us dancing at the Patio Club. As newlyweds, Jeri and Danny rented an apartment on Jerome Avenue and 108th Street. One time they had unexpected company and Danny came over and quickly asked Mom if she had any scotch. Liquor was frowned upon and kept hidden, so Mom dug out a bottle of scotch, which was way back on a closet shelf. It was like excavating a mine! When he came home from work, Mom mentioned to Dad that Danny needed a bottle of scotch, and he asked what she gave him. Dad cringed when she naively answered, “Oh, I gave him some Puerto Rican junk—a bottle of Chivas Regal.”

Mom and Dad regretted letting Reenie go to nursing school in Yonkers, because she didn’t come home very much and seemed to be drifting away from the family. They were concerned, and quite often Bill and I would drive them to Yonkers to see Reenie and remind her that we missed her. She seemed content in her surroundings, but we weren’t letting go of her! A few times Bill and Mom drove up alone to visit Reenie to see how she was doing. Bill, sworn to secrecy by Mom, wouldn’t tell me a thing (not that much was happening). He and Mom were very much alike. You could threaten to cut out their tongues, cut off their arms and legs, and throw them off a cliff—they weren't talking! Quiet of nature and never one for pomposity, Reenie came home one weekend with Tom Leak, the man she married unannounced on December 5, 1964—no reception, no shower, no fuss. We were all shocked but accepted the fact that Reenie chose to do this. The important thing was that Reenie was back with the family again! Tom was a plumber, Reenie a nurse, and for a while they lived in Richmond Hill. They eventually moved to New Rochelle and proceeded to have four wonderful sons—Tommy, Michael, Robert, and Kevin.

The 1960s were a tumultuous time in America. The very unpopular Vietnam War was in full swing, and anti-war protests and flag burnings were everywhere. With Mom and Dad, all of us were the biggest flag wavers at any parades that were held in support of America's troops. NOW—the National Organization for Women—was founded in 1966, and bras were thrown out or burned in the name of freedom. Flower people were everywhere, calling for free love and peace, and were against the conventional ways of our country. Drugs—pot, heroin, LSD, and more—were prevalent in the hippie movement and music of the time. President John Kennedy was assassinated in 1963, as were his brother Robert Kennedy and Martin Luther King in 1968. Violence and liberal protests against the war caused utter chaos throughout America's colleges and institutions of learning. Our country was in complete turmoil. America survived—but would never be the same. It was a tough time to raise kids and keep family traditions.

Dad was still working two full-time jobs, and Mom was still holding down the fort—each lonely, I'm sure, for the other's company. Precious time was always taken for each other, with their enjoyable bus trips and their evenings at the Rathskeller in Ridgewood, where they dined and danced. George had a car and quite often took my parents for scenic rides along the Delaware Water Gap, which they totally enjoyed.

I couldn't resist the opportunity to work at the 1964/65 World's Fair in Flushing Meadow. Fran worked at the Bell Telephone display, and I was hired at the Clairol Pavilion. I loved it—especially having a free pass to take Bill, Mom, Dad, and my brothers and sisters to see the whole shebang, without waiting in long lines! With the passing of time, George and Peggy's firstborn, Stephen, was joined by five brothers and sisters—Michael, Terry, Patty, Kenneth, and Raymond. Dolores and Don had Don Jr., Doreen, and Denise. Jeri and Danny had a son, Daniel Jr., who later became big brother to Patrick, Andrea, and Corinne. In October 1965, Bill was working in a print shop in Ozone Park, and I was working at the World's Fair when we moved to a lovely five-room apartment on 89th Street in Ozone Park—because I was finally pregnant!

Our beautiful blonde-haired, blue-eyed son, William Jr. (Billy), was born December 20, 1965, in Mary Immaculate Hospital, Jamaica. He was the best Christmas gift we ever received! Reenie and Tom, who were living in Richmond Hill at the time, had their firstborn—Tommy Jr.—the next day, on December 21, at Queens General Hospital. Jeri gave birth to Patrick on December 30 at Wycoff Heights Hospital in Forest Hills, where Dolores was also a patient due to bursitis in her knee. Needless to say, my parents were doing a lot of running around and somehow were there for everybody. Mom, to be sure, did the customary counting of fingers and toes and checked for flat ears on all her new grandsons. Unexpectedly, Mom and Dad's hospital visits weren't quite over.

A few days after Billy was born I hemorrhaged and returned to the hospital. Bill told me later that my mother was very upset that he had signed papers giving permission for a hysterectomy to be done if the bleeding didn't stop. She felt that hysterectomies were done unnecessarily and too often without reason enough. What did Bill know? He was young, scared, a nervous new father, and did what the doctors suggested might be necessary. Thank God all turned out well. When I went for follow-up X-rays, it was discovered I had a double uterus, which caused the problem and made me realize—boy, *I'm a mess!*

I loved walking with my baby in a carriage, and my sisters and I would meet and spend our time shopping at Liberty or Jamaica Avenues. Believe it or not, in those days, we left our babies outside in the carriage while we went grocery shopping. It was a different world compared to today. The loving couple we rented from, Caroline and Luco, treated us like family and always sent up delicious Italian food leftovers because I was "too skinny." Our Billy, their "pretty boy," kids to this day that his cheeks are still sore from being tweaked by them!

Bill and I were saving to buy a house. Bill worked three jobs to do so—his regular printing job, Pizza City on Crossbay Boulevard (leftovers were great!), and the *New York* Times on weekends. With Dad's influence, he and my brothers and brothers-in-law earned a good night's pay working at the *New York Times* for extra money. Since Billy ate baby food and Bill grabbed a meal between jobs, I got kind of lax about eating, and at 5' 9" weighed 109 lbs. When we saw Fran, who was still doing the singles scene, she said if I closed one eye I'd look like a needle and told Bill not to let me wear a black dress if we went out to dinner, because the waiter would ask him to check his umbrella. Dolores and Mom said I was too pale and thin and encouraged me to go for a checkup. Turned out I was anemic—shots cleared it up, and I was back to normal.

It was house-buying time! The whole family was on the move!

Dolores and Don had bought a house in Woodhaven, Jeri and Danny bought a house on Long Island, George and Peggy bought a house in Queens, and we bought a house in Woodhaven. I hate to break the news to house hunters today, but the average going prices at that time in the '60s were $20,000. After sweating through the closing, hoping we had enough money for everything, Bill and I were shocked to find that the old couple we bought the house from had taken every light bulb, outlet, and switch cover with them. Already it was costing us to be homeowners!

Chapter 15

Mom and Dad finally got a phone! Ray needed one to receive calls for his NYPD job. In 1968, *Mom got her driver's license!* She and Ray, now 18 with a new license, split the cost of a $400 Ford Fairlane. Mom then went to auto mechanic classes so she would be knowledgeable and not get ripped off if something was wrong with the car! Always on the alert! They agreed that Mom would use the car during the week, and Ray would have it on weekends. *Yeah, right!* With her new independence, Vera was on the move! Five Towns Shopping Center, John's Bargain Store, E. J. Korvettes, Jamaica, Green Acres Mall—there was no stopping her! She and Dad would pack the car with grandkids and take them to amusement parks, or show up at everybody's houses to share the great bargains they found.

Dad seemed to have no interest in getting a driver's license and enjoyed being chauffeured around. He was a fun Grandpa. Usually every Sunday, *before the stores were allowed to be opened for shopping on this treasured family day*, we all congregated at Mom and Dad's, and somehow there was always enough food to feed everyone. The grandchildren would have a great time—especially when they tried to sneak into Grandpa's room while he was sleeping. You see, Grandpa always had candy bars under his pillow for this purpose! He was the "gorilla," and the kids were his little "monkeys." They would quietly approach snoring Grandpa and try to reach under his pillow. Gorilla would mumble, toss and turn, and hold his pillow, and the monkeys would back off a bit. When another attempt was made for the candy, Gorilla would pop up and roar and joyful giggles were heard as the gorilla and his monkeys embraced in hugs, kisses, and laughter—and the monkeys got their candy! As hard as he worked, as tired as he was, Dad always had a wonderful sense of humor and enjoyed all his little monkeys.

Lorraine had a job at Nestles Co. and was against giving a portion of her pay toward the "house." The breakdown was in thirds—savings, house, self. The arguments were weekly but ended when Lorraine Upton and Erich Weiss, who also worked at Nestles, got married at St. Bennies on May 26, 1968. Lorraine looked absolutely beautiful with her handsome husband, who was so thin we all kidded that if it got windy he'd better put rocks in his pockets to hold him down! Their reception was at the Patio Club. Erich was born in Austria, and the hired band played a lot of polkas and ooom-pah-pah music. I went up and requested an Irish song, and Jeri and I got out on the dance floor and did the Irish jig. My father was proudly watching and happily clapping his hands, as was his Irish family. Jeri and I laughed our heads off later since we didn't know how to jig; we just winged it and put on a good show! Lorraine's wedding, as all of ours, was paid for in cash by our hardworking Dad and penny-saving Mom. Erich was transferred to Massachusetts, and the newlyweds moved there. They proceeded to have a lovely family—Christine, Karen, Erich Jr., Erinn, and David, and still live there to this day.

Bill and I wanted to have our children close in age, but it just wasn't happening. My menstrual cycle was always erratic—twenty days, ninety days, forty days, etc.—but my ob-gyn doctor didn't seem concerned. Finally, when Billy was almost 3, I got pregnant again and was absolutely elated. Once at Dolores's house when I was pregnant, all the nieces and nephews were running around playing hide-and-seek when little Denise ran by, picked up my maternity top, kissed my belly, and said "Hi, baby—I love you!" Grandma Wolf was sitting there and was shocked and thought it "vas deesgusting dat the child shuut know dat." Due July 21, our baby arrived a month later—well worth the wait! Wanting to look good and be prepared, I shaved my legs so much I thought I'd hit bone! August 18, 1969, our beautiful, blonde-haired, blue-eyed Michele was born. When looking out my hospital window, I saw Billy outside with his Uncle Eddie. He yelled up five stories, "Did the baby come out yet, Mommy?" Shortly after, I heard the pitter patter of little feet, and 3 1/2 year-old Billy appeared! Eddie was right behind him, claiming, "Billy was so smart he found the staircase to the fifth floor." Amazing! Billy loved meeting his new sister.

Michele was baptized on Labor Day weekend—the same day our street was having a block party. 91st Avenue was closed to traffic between 86th and 87th Streets, and everyone invited and fed their family and friends from noon until midnight. Big Wheel races, games for the kids, cotton candy, and ice cream were in abundance, and there was dancing in the street for everyone. Fireworks wound down a fun day for all. Baby Michele was content being Catholic and slept through the whole thing.

I was always, and still am, a beach lover. I feel close to God when I view the ocean's expanse. I am in awe of God's power and wonder about the mysteries of the sea and the history it holds. I used to take Billy and Michele to the beach all the time, no matter what the season. They'd play with a pail and shovel in the sand or surrounded by a blanket of snow sometimes, we'd walk along the boardwalk and listen to the waves pounding the shore beneath the blue-gray, seemingly hand-brushed skies created by God. In the summer, I took Tommy, Adrianne, nieces and nephews, and anyone who could cram into the car, along with the beach ball, pails, and shovels, to Rockaway Beach. One of my nephews once told me he wouldn't be such a beach lover if it wasn't for those trips.

My favorite beach was on 130th Street in Belle Harbor, past the blanket city of beach 116. Parking was restricted, and I'd drive around until I found a legal spot. It was well worth the effort; Belle Harbor was quiet, much less crowded, and totally enjoyable. My idea of enjoying the beach is quite simple: toss on a bathing suit, grab a towel and some goodies to eat and drink, and go! When Dolores went I always had a good laugh. She brought everything but the kitchen sink for her kids to eat, and when it came time to leave it was a riot. I would tell Billy and Michele to come out of the water, dry off, shake off the sand, and we'd go home and take a shower. Well, Dolores sat Don Jr., Doreen, and Denise on a bench, wrapped them in a towel, and changed them into a fresh outfit after removing their bathing suits and every granule of sand. The best part was when she cleaned their feet with a towel, making sure to remove every grain of sand between "dere widdle toesies." I waited and continued tanning. Believe me, sandy or not, a fun day was had by all!

In December 1969, when most of our family and friends were relocating to Long Island, Dolores and Don moved upstate to Pearl River, New York. Bill and I were very close to them, and our Billy was like a little brother to their kids. The McGuire home in Woodhaven was always open to all the family, and Don and Dolores were the common sense, get-good-advice couple who seemingly had it all together. Dolores was a mentor, confidante, and advisor to me and my sisters. We all loved Don like a brother, and he was always there if someone had a problem. One of my brothers said someone once asked him, "If your father was so busy working two full-time jobs, who taught you to be a man?" He thought for a second and said, "My brothers-in-law—Don

McGuire and Bill Stamm." With the McGuires now in Pearl River, the Stamm household in Woodhaven became the hub of family activities.

Life is full of surprises, as Bill and I soon discovered being new homeowners. At three months old, Michele was diagnosed with congenital hip dysplasia; the gas heater furnace died and had to be replaced; and Bill lost his job. *Oy vey!* Michele's hip problem was corrected by wearing a freja splint for a year, learning to crawl, walk, and ride a Big Wheel while doing so. If the condition had not been discovered, one leg would have been shorter and she would have limped. With money borrowed from Mom and Dad, we drove to New Jersey, bought a complete gas heating unit, and Bill, his brother John, and my brother Robert installed it. Mom, always a believer in the importance of education, strongly urged Bill to use his VA benefits to go to school to learn computers, which were the up-and-coming thing. Mom knew he was smart and encouraged him, knowing he would do well. Bill, who felt downtrodden with our financial situation, had never given VA financing a thought. He received his Computer Degree in December 1970 and immediately got a job as a computer programmer at a hospital in Brooklyn. He loved entering this new world of computers and really excelled in it—and does to this day.

One day I got a call from Fran, still single, saying she was coming to spend the night at our house in Woodhaven. The bell rang, I opened the door, and there she nonchalantly stood—with a shopping bag in hand and the head of a shaven pig sticking out of it! She said she stopped in China Town to pick up a pig and was taking it to her Aunt Frances in Floral Park, who always wanted to have a luau. Billy and Michele were already asleep, so Fran and I sat up half the night talking and laughing, as always. Before we went to bed, she propped the pig up and centered it on the kitchen table, put an apple in its mouth, and left it there for the kids to discover. In the morning, the kids went down to the kitchen and saw the pig, and Billy loudly exclaimed, *"Fran's here!"* Billy and Michele always loved Fran and knew something exciting would take place whenever she visited. I heard the luau was a success and left her Aunt Frances as happy as a pig in mud!

Mom and Dad always stressed the importance of married couples getting away alone once in a while. I loved having Tommy and Adrianne stay at our house when Mom and Dad went away. Tommy enjoyed being with Bill, and I loved fussing and primping with Adrianne. Having so many brothers and sisters was great and gave all of us the opportunity to get away for a weekend without a worry about babysitters. We would watch each other's kids while weekend getaways were taken in the Poconos, Catskills, Atlantic City, or wherever. With the everyday hustle bustle of raising a family, it was important to get away and recall, "Hey—weren't you the one in the white gown?" "Yeah—weren't you the one in the tuxedo?"

Chapter 16

Mom always asked Dad to work less so they could have more time together, but Dad wasn't ready to stop working. Dennis, Robert, Tommy, and Adrianne were still going to school when Mom decided to get a job. She first started working a night job at the post office in Jamaica and then got a full-time position at Social Security in Rego Park. She loved it—and Dad hated it. Dad felt deeply hurt and insulted that his wife went to work, after all the years he had been the hardworking sole provider of his ever-growing family. There was no financial reason for Mom to go to work. Mom, on the other hand, was a smart, organized woman who wanted to prove she was capable of being a loving mother while holding down a job. They argued a lot about it. Dad's hurt came across as anger, and Mom's wanting to prove herself was portrayed as undaunted stubbornness. Neither one "won." The communication wasn't there for Dad to say, "Vera, I love you, and feel deeply hurt, embarrassed, unneeded, and stripped of my manhood by you going to work." And Mom didn't know how to say, "George, I love you and appreciate all your hard work, but I have a brain too, and am capable of much more than just doing housework." Unfortunately, Dad packed his bags and stayed at his friend Al's house for about a week, and Mom and the kids were devastated.

My younger brothers tell me that when Dad moved out, he came over the house every day and quietly sat on the stoop as they played ball or other games in the street. They didn't realize then, as kids, that he came to see them, and they just continued playing. Growing up and looking back, they feel bad that they didn't recognize Daddy's loneliness and need to be with them.

Hindsight is wonderful, but sometimes can be, "If only I had known, I would have …"

I felt so helpless when this was happening and went to speak to the priest at St. Bennies, looking for some guidance, direction, and hopefully some help from the church. Crying, I told the priest what was happening to my parents and begged him to intervene and talk to them. He said the situation was very sad, but that *the church had no right to interfere with anyone's marriage!* Interfere? How about helping! I thought I was hearing things! I asked him if this was the same church that professed that marriage was a lifetime commitment and spoke from the pulpit about propagation of the faith by producing children. The same church that was now saying *no* to the problems of my parents who produced and steadfastly raised twelve Catholic children. The priest was speechless after I proclaimed my disappointment and frustration—and I quietly left.

Mom and Dad worked things out and were back together again, as affectionate and loving as always. (No thanks to the church.) Dad continued working two jobs, and Mom loved driving to her job at Social Security. She used to tell us of her co-workers who would receive a complaint or problem from SS clients and just throw it in the garbage. Mom made a point of delving into the issue and getting the right answers for those hardworking Americans. Meanwhile, Dennis graduated from NY School of Printing and joined the navy, and Robert graduated from Bishop Loughlin HS and entered the marines. Even though the Vietnam War was still taking place, neither of them was actively involved in it. Tommy graduated from St. Bennies and went to Delehanty High School in Jamaica. Adrianne was still in St. Bennies, getting a little frisky, and kept Mom busy driving around to check on her friends and activities.

Chapter 17

In 1971, *love was in the air*—and my brothers were bitten by the bug! On July 26, 1971, Edward Upton and his sweetheart Mary were married at St. Fortunatas church in Brooklyn. Dad looked so handsome in his black-trimmed white tuxedo, dancing with Mom in her floral gown with red flowers. Eddie worked for the airlines, Mary was a secretary, and they became a family when they were blessed with their beautiful children, Peter and Carolyn. Due to Eddie's continued schooling and vice presidential airline positions, they lived in California, New York, Minnesota, Connecticut, and eventually Florida. Raymond Upton married beautiful Diane Crosby—a former classmate of Eddie's—at St. Bennies on November 27, 1971. Mom looked so elegant in her velvet-topped, floral-bottomed gown dancing with Dad in his black tuxedo. Dennis was in his navy uniform, Robert in his marine uniform, as handsomely suited Tommy danced with Adrianne in her polka-dotted dress. Grandma Wolf—now 81—loved being surrounded by the family. Ray and Diane's love shines through their four beautiful children—Deborah, Laura, Brian, and Donna. Pleased with the choice of their new daughters-in-law, Mom and Dad looked so happy at both weddings (maybe too, after five daughters' weddings, they were happy they didn't have to pick up the tab!)

The love bug was also in Oakdale. Fran and Mansukh (Manu) were married September 25, 1971. I once wrote a story about Fran, describing her as "the Auntie Mame of my life," never knowing what to expect. Manu, a tall, thin Indian man wearing a grey suit, looked so handsome and distinguished with his black hair, sideburns, and mustache. Fran, in her white, gold-trimmed sari, long red silk scarf draped over one shoulder, and a bead on her forehead, looked beautiful. With her black hair, she looked more Indian than Manu! St. Lawrence Catholic Church in Sayville was filled with Fran's very conservative, Irish-Catholic relatives, and on the altar were four black gospel singers, as "Let It Be" echoed throughout the church. I poked Bill and said, "She did it again!" The wedding was followed by a blast of a reception held at Dowling College in Oakdale, where Fran's mother was a staff member. Fran and Manu lived in Canada, and still do, where they raised their wonderful daughter and son, Juthika (Juti) and Tarun.

The love bug was still active when Bill and I, after much hesitancy, made a Marriage Encounter weekend on October 21, 1971, right before our ninth anniversary. We heard it was for good marriages to be made better, but the word "encounter" made us leery. In the '60s and '70s, the meaning of the word was the touchy-feely free-love stuff that went on with the hippies and flower people. It turned out to be a very private and personal experience for each couple there, as we had been assured. Marriage Encounter is a weekend that becomes a lifetime of sharing feelings and deepening marital communication with your life partner. As deeply in love as we were already, after the wonderful weekend together, Bill and I knew the best was yet to be. We are grateful to this day for Marriage Encounter, which opened our hearts and souls to deeper communication and spirituality in our life together. We wanted every married couple we knew to experience this!

Danny and Jeri went to ME before us, then Eddie and Mary, Dolores and Don, and various friends made a Marriage Encounter weekend, and we offered it as a gift to Mom and Dad. We were so excited when they left on Friday for the weekend but disappointed on Sunday night when they returned to say they had gone to Atlantic City instead. Mom said on Saturday morning when breakfast was served they only had orange juice—and didn't have pineapple juice that Daddy liked. So they left and went to Atlantic City. *Bull!* Dad could have cared less about pineapple juice! I knew immediately that the decision was Mom's, and that she was shrewd enough to see that the weekend—sharing inner feelings from your heart and soul—made her feel uneasy and hesitant to stay. Bill and I felt bad, because we knew Mom and Dad would benefit from it. But thank goodness they did fine without it.

Chapter 18

Mom and Dad agreed that Richmond Hill was changing and started looking at houses elsewhere. In August 1972, the Richmond Hill Uptons moved to Franklin Square. It was an unforgettable experience! Bill and I stopped over the house the night before the move and were surprised to find Mom calmly drinking her coffee while reading the newspaper. There wasn't a sign of preparation for the move. Not a thing was packed, nor a cardboard box to be found. Dad was working, the movers were coming at noon the next day, and obviously Mom, usually very organized, didn't know where to begin. I started by taking everything on the dressers and rolling it into the scarf that lay on top, then put it in the top drawer of each one. Dressers—ready to move! Bill got as many boxes as he could for packing and called work to say he wouldn't be in the next day. I called friends who said Billy and Michele could stay at their house for as long as necessary.

Bill and I arrived early on moving day with more boxes and got right to work. While Bill and Tommy were taking the beds apart and packing everything in the living room and bedrooms, I started packing the kitchen dishes, pots, pans, and silverware when Mom said not to because Adrianne, now 12, hadn't eaten breakfast yet. Well, tough! I gave Adrianne $2 and told her to go to Jean's candy store and get a bagel and hot chocolate. I wrapped the dishes in old newspapers, used rubber bands to gather the silverware, and boxed the tons of canned food in the cabinets and pantry. Everything in the refrigerator was put in coolers. The clothes, shoes, boots, gloves, framed pictures, and paraphernalia seemed unending, as each box was labeled as best as possible.

The movers arrived at noon, after doing a small moving job in the morning. They figured two small moving jobs in one day. Well, it seems Mom, thinking she would get a bargain, told the moving company she had a five-room apartment. Actually there were six rooms, a bathroom, an alcove, and a full pantry. Mom also "forgot to mention" the full basement and garage, filled to capacity with memorabilia from her twelve children! Bill, Tommy, and I pitched in to help the weary movers. Adrianne didn't help much. Well into the night we were carrying boxes from the room in the basement—games, fold-up chairs, cartons of books, magazines, tools, prom dresses and evening wear from five daughters, cartons of sixteen-ounce cans of Columbian coffee—purchased on sale for 69¢. Bikes, wagons, baby carriage, shovels, and all sorts of stuff were pulled from the garage. Finally—in the dark—everything was moved to Franklin Square to be unloaded. Again, Bill, Tommy, and I helped the movers, everyone exhausted.

I helped Mom set up the kitchen, while Bill and Tommy put the beds and furniture together. I went back the next day to unload the boxes and do whatever had to be done. Eventually all was settled into place. I don't know what the move cost, but it was no bargain for anyone, especially the misled movers. Mom was extremely thankful for our help and kept saying she couldn't have done it without us. We didn't disagree. Although not funny at the time, through the years we all had a good laugh over moving day. Looking back, I realize what an overwhelming task the move was for Mom and how totally helpless she must have felt.

The house on Ribbon Street was a pretty one, with a nice fenced-in front lawn and garden. There was a second-floor apartment. The living room had two fully mirrored walls and newly purchased furniture, and the eat-in kitchen was comfortable with a side entrance to the driveway, backyard, and garage. There was only one *bathroom* on the first floor, but no big lines! There was a thousand-gallon oil tank for heating, and Mom took full advantage of that. Always careful of how money was spent, Mom contacted various oil companies, told them of the exceptionally big oil tank, and dealt with the lowest bidders. When the oil trucks came to deliver, she wisely ordered a few hundred gallons from one and a few hundred gallons from the other companies for the remaining amount. They all kept lowering the price per gallon, vying for the business of filling a thousand-gallon oil tank. Mom and Dad won the competition by saving a lot of money!

Adrianne had her own room (what's that?) with a huge globe light over her bed, which was a pullout for when she had friends over. Tommy's room was in the basement, very private, and had plenty of room for all his sports equipment and stereo. It must have been difficult for each of them to move so far away from their friends. Adrianne, 12, was enrolled in St. Catherine's Catholic School, and Tommy, 15, switched from Delehanty HS to Carey HS in Franklin Square. He was tall and handsome—eventually 6'5" - and became quite the football player. Tommy had long, shoulder-length blonde hair, an "in" style in the '60s and '70s, and Dad didn't like it at all and razzed him about it. Tommy and Adrianne grew very close, being the only ones living at home. Adrianne, who missed her friends, was against moving from Richmond Hill and made no bones about it. Ironically, having moved to a nicer neighborhood, Mom kept driving back to Richmond Hill to do shopping in her old haunts. She couldn't resist returning to Liberty and Jamaica Avenues, Jamaica, City Line (Brooklyn/Queens border), and bumping into old neighbors. She also took Adrianne to visit her friends while she did so, although she was leery about it.

I'll never forget the night Mom, Dad, and Tommy came to

our house in Woodhaven. Adrianne had run away. Mom and Dad were crying their eyes out, heartbroken thinking maybe they shouldn't have moved. It broke my heart to realize my parents, now in their late fifties and early sixties, had to deal with teenagers during these volatile times. Bill and I cradled them in our arms to console them. Tommy was mad as heck and said he was going to go to Adrianne's friends' houses and kick butt. Bill said he was going with him—to make sure he didn't kick butt! Tommy stood outside her friends' houses and said, "Come on out Adrianne. I know you're in there!" and eventually it paid off. Exhausted, but relieved, Mom, Dad, Tommy, and unhappy Adrianne all quietly went home.

Bill and I and the kids, and some of our other brothers and sisters, enjoyed going to Tommy's football games. We could spot Mom a mile away. Her protective umbrella was a landmark on a hot, sunny day. Being Mom was in her late fifties, she was very happy when we "younger ones" showed up with her for the games to cheer Tommy on. She was conscious of being older than his friends' parents and felt more accepted as "one of the crowd" when we were all there. We had done the same when my brothers who were Boy Scouts were in canoeing races in Jamaica Bay. We enjoyed being there for everything. It was just another great opportunity to be together as family.

When Christmas rolled around, it was obvious that the family was too big to have the Christmas party at Mom and Dad's, so Bill and I started having it in our basement in Woodhaven. Santa came jingling down the stairs, much to the delight of the awaiting little ones perched on our six-foot coffee table. Babies and toddlers all over the place! One Christmas Santa held three newborns in his arms! Grandma Wolf tasted the potato salad I made and *knew* I grated the onion instead of dicing it. Tsk! Tsk!

As Christmas songs were sung and gifts exchanged, Mom and Dad were in their glory being surrounded by their children and grandchildren—especially knowing they didn't have to clean up! The older, wiser kids would check out Santa's shoes, watch, hair, etc., for clues as to who Santa really was. We all caught on, and to this day Santa has big black boots, a red velvet suit, and a very authentic big white beard and wig. We still see some curious little eyes wondering if it's really "him."

In 1973, Dad was not feeling well and looked pale and tired, and went to the doctor. He was told he was in jeopardy of having a heart attack and was advised to take a cab immediately to the hospital. Of course, he *walked* to Jamaica Hospital from Metropolitan Avenue. He was admitted for a few days, released, and continued working. Shortly after, Mom slipped on ice when getting off the elevator at the Social Security office where she worked and fractured her spine as a result. She was in a wheelchair and devastated to be so restrained. Dennis got married in March 1974, and Mom was mortified to be in a wheelchair for the occasion. Dad wheeled around his strong-willed, freedom-seeking, restricted Vera who was determined to heal and get back into life's activities—which she did. She never went back to work but was back to driving all over the place. Dennis and his wife moved to Arizona, where he worked at the newspaper. They divorced, but Dennis has a beautiful daughter, Sharon, and still lives in Arizona. Robert married and moved to Arizona also, where his lovely daughter, Barbie Jean, was born. He and his wife divorced, and Robert moved back to New York, working at the *New York Times*. He married again years later.

Still working at the *New York Times*, Daddy retired from West Chemical in 1975, allowing him more time to spend at home. Being everyone was married and out of the house, Tommy and Adrianne were fortunate to have what some of us didn't—a closer relationship with Mom and Dad. Mom loved talking with Tommy about stocks, bonds, real estate, and investments, encouraging him to watch the stock market. It paid off! When Tommy—and my brothers and brothers-in-law—worked a shift at the *New York Times*, they had the chance to spend more time with Dad. The camaraderie was good, and Dad didn't have to take the bus and trains home. His sons drove him! Adrianne had very special time with Mom. She shared her dreams of modeling, becoming a movie star, and traveling, and Mom enjoyed listening to her. Beautiful Adrianne and handsome Tommy, both poised with excellent posture, had portfolios put together and did some modeling and TV commercials.

When Adrianne was 15 years old, all of us sisters—except Adrianne—were sitting around Mom's kitchen table talking and having our coffee. Since Mom and Dad had airline privileges from both George and Eddie, I asked where they were planning to go on vacation. Mom said they were going to Hawaii.

Me: "Mom, why Hawaii? You hate the beach."

Mom: "Well, Adrianne hasn't worn her new bathing suit on Waikiki Beach."

With that, I reached into my purse, grabbed some tissues, and handed them out to my chuckling sisters, fictitiously dabbing my eyes while declaring how sad it was that Adrianne hadn't worn her new bathing suit on Waikiki Beach. Mom sat there with a knowing grin on her face.

Reenie: "What's Waikiki Beach?"

Me: "Never mind that—what's a new bathing suit?"

Needless to say, we were all laughing hysterically, including Mom. Obviously, things had changed a *lot*. We went on the Staten Island Ferry for a nickel, and Adrianne was going to Hawaii!

Adrianne always said she felt like she had six mothers while growing up, with each of us sisters giving her different advice along the way. She used to take a lot of razzing from her brothers, too, and sometimes didn't know how to handle it. Adrianne wasn't too quick with the comebacks, even though I tried teaching her. One time Tommy said, "Adrianne, notice Mommy and Daddy stopped having kids after *you* were born?" Adrianne looked pathetically frantic at me for an answer. I said I knew why, and Tommy rolled his eyes and said, "Why, big sister?" I simply said that Mommy and Daddy were striving for perfection, and when Adrianne was born they sighed, "Ah—finally!" Being the youngest, she was an innocent target. Another time my younger brothers were really giving her a hard time and she was on the verge of crying. I took my brothers aside and reminded them that, since I was their older sister, when they were small I used to tend to their personal needs. I told them that even though the Constitution says all men are created equal, I knew otherwise—and could blow the whistle at any time. I left them with something to think about and a reminder to leave Adrianne alone!

Grandma Wolf, getting on in years, participated in any and all family functions. One day, while trimming the hedges, she had a stroke and was hospitalized. Once home again, Aunt Julia, who lived downstairs, took good care of her. I went over and helped with the housekeeping, making sure the floors were scrubbed and cleaned to Grandma's high expectations. I helped Aunt Julia bathe her, and I knew, except for the results of the stroke, this very dignified lady would be mortified knowing her granddaughter saw her naked and without her false teeth. Unfortunately, while being helped to go outside one day, Grandma fell down the stairs and broke her hip. She spent many years at Trump Pavilion for

Nursing and Rehabilitation in Richmond Hill and was well taken care of because she always had constant visitors.

As time passed my father's family had a few deaths, and naturally Mom and Dad helped other family members clear out the belongings in the house or apartment of the deceased relative. In the process, my parents came across letters that were written by my father's family—the Upton women—that went back and forth to each other through the years. They were letters about my mother being Lutheran. Evidently they were keeping watch to make sure "Vera was keeping up her end of the bargain" and raising the children Catholic as promised. *Hello?* Can anybody count? Mom and Dad had twelve children and sacrificed and paid tuition for our Catholic school educations. I don't recall any of these good Catholic letter writers having large families or coming anywhere near to accomplishing what my parents did.

Chapter 19

Since Lorraine and Erich lived in Massachusetts, it became the center of winter fun for the whole family. Billy and Michele loved to go there and have fun with their cousins in the snow, and Bill and I loved thawing out with Lorraine and Erich over a good game of cards. They had a beautiful high ranch in a lovely treed area, and Bill and I started looking at the real estate listings. We couldn't believe the beautiful houses for sale at half the price or less than in New York. Long story short, Bill got a computer job at a bank in West Springfield. We rented a beautiful, huge three-bedroom townhouse in Westfield (west of West Springfield) and enrolled Billy, 9, and Michele, 7 in Holy Trinity Catholic School in time for September classes. We sold the house in Woodhaven, and our plans were set for the move to Massachusetts.

I'll never forget the day—August 22, 1975—when Ray called at 6:30 AM to say Danny Kline, Jeri's husband, had been killed in a car accident while driving home from his job at the New York City sanitation department. The whole family was numb with disbelief. Although neither was familiar with the protocol, Bill and Eddie helped with the funeral arrangements and chose a cemetery plot. Danny Jr., 10, Patrick 9, Andrea 5 and Corinne 4 were held in the arms of their gentle, loving, heartbroken mother. I wanted to rescind our plans to move to Massachusetts, but we couldn't. Thank God Mom and Dad lived near Jeri and were helpful and supportive. Don and Dolores shared their love, advice, and consolation. Bill helped Jeri with the finances and paperwork, which he went over with her whenever we came down from Massachusetts. Ray, Eddie, Robert, and Tommy were there to help. The whole family pitched in. Jeri, 30 at the time, worked tenaciously her whole life; her heart and soul always devoted to her children and their safe and secure upbringing. She selflessly raised them alone better than most families with two parents. Jeri got her driver's license, and with Bill as her coach, drove safely and successfully to Massachusetts. It was her first of many long-distance trips. Accepting and dealing with every challenge along the way, Jeri is a very loving, knowledgeable, and confident woman today. We are all proud of Jeri for her unending hard work and accomplishments through the years.

At age 33, before we moved to Massachusetts, I had not menstruated for a year. I thought maybe I was going through early menopause and asked Mom when she went through change-of-life. Of course her response was, "I don't think I ever did." So I decided to go to a doctor for the answer. The city was changing, and doctors were selling their medical practices to Indian, Oriental, or other foreign doctors—unfamiliar to me as I was to them. I didn't know what was wrong, except to say, "I wasn't me." Usually pretty happy-go-lucky, I would cry or get upset for no known reason. One Indian gynecologist told me, "If it is attention you are looking for, I can send you to an endocrinologist in Manhattan and you can spend thousands of dollars for attention." Little did he know.

Moving day arrived, and my brothers were a big help filling the rented truck. Mom was there, crying when we were ready to leave, yet assuring us it was a good move. Tommy drove to Massachusetts with Bill in the moving truck, and I followed with Billy and Michele in the car. I understand Bill and Tommy had quite a good conversation about Tommy's future and which direction he should go. Although Mom was always giving him wise and informed advice, Tommy, who was always smart and knowledgeable about finances, said he looked to Bill as his "guiding light." I'm happy to this day that Tommy was with us to empty the moving truck and help put all the furniture together, as was Lorraine's husband Erich when we got to Westfield, Massachusetts.

Once settled in our new townhouse, I ended up seeing a highly regarded Springfield gynecologist, Dr. James Fitz, who sent me for skull X-rays. It was discovered I had a tumor on my pituitary gland, resulting in a hormone imbalance, and I was given the name of a neurosurgeon to call. I was given an appointment a month away. I was a wreck and knew I couldn't wait that long. Let's face it, you hear tumor, you think cancer—you think death. I couldn't sleep, eat, or function for two days. Who was going to take care of Bill and the kids? I wouldn't be there to see them grow up! Suppose I ended up being incapacitated? Fearful and worried, I was given the name of a new neurosurgeon in Springfield, Dr. Peter Gold, who saw me in two days.

Dr. Gold saw us for four hours on his day off and immediately informed us that we were neighbors. I was from Richmond Hill, and he was from Forest Hills. I quickly reminded him of the railroad tracks that ran between and separated the rich Jewish side and the poor Christian side. We were off to a flying start! He assured us that pituitary tumors were usually 99.9 % benign, and proceeded to give us every detail of the surgery and the endocrinology (hormone) workup involved. He told us that the tumor, causing a hormone imbalance, was why I had such whacked up periods and difficulty getting pregnant, and said that we were fortunate to have any children. (In jest, I have reminded Billy and Michele how lucky they are to be here!)

We explained as gently and honestly as possible to Billy, 10 and Michele, 7 that a growth had to be removed from Mommy's brain, knowing they would hear neighbors and friends discussing it. A very big concern was how to tell Mom and Dad. Since Mom had TB when she carried me, I was very aware of the fact that she'd have a guilt trip and blame herself big time. *No way* was I going to allow that. One day while talking to Jeri on the phone, explaining the diagnosis and my concern for Mom, Mom walked in her house. She got on the phone and I carefully explained what was happening. Mom asked where the pituitary gland was, and I said that it was behind the sinuses. I totally avoided the word "brain" and said growth instead of tumor. She asked if it's something you're born with, and I emphatically answered *no*—that the doctor had no idea what causes these growths, and that they are extremely slow growing and benign. (True.) Thank goodness Jeri was there with her nursing experience and medical books to explain as best she could what was involved after we got off the phone.

Of course I was thinking, "I just left the biggest and best city in the world for medical attention. What am I doing here in Massachusetts?" All through this ordeal we were receiving loving and concerned phone calls from my brothers and sisters and were thankful for the Irish sense of humor. "Let's face it—we all knew your problems were in your head." "Mommy said when you were a baby you fell out of the crib on your head." "It all started when you were hit in the head with a baseball." "That's why you're called Batty Patty." My only comeback was that at least I had X-rays to prove I had a brain! And Lorraine, who lived nearby and didn't deal with this stuff too well, was probably thinking, "Oh my God! Did she have to move to Massachusetts?"

While getting a second opinion at NY University Hospital we were told the diagnosis and surgical procedure was correct, and that Dr. Gold was a highly rated neurosurgeon. I was hospitalized for two weeks of pre-surgical X-rays. (That's why I'm so radiant!) I told Dr. Gold that I wanted to know everything that was going on, and he obliged by being open, detailed, and descriptive about all procedures. He told me that a pneumoencephalogram would be the final and most painful test and would result in my staying quietly in bed for a few days after. I found out why. Picture an electric chair. While completely strapped in the chair and totally immovable, the spinal fluid was removed and replaced with air to separate the brain for detailed X-rays. The chair then lifted and swung around in all directions—up, down, sideways, upside down—while X-rays were taken. (Almost like some amusement rides—but *no fun!*) The air stirring in the head was what caused the extreme pain. Dr. Gold said I was doing excellent, and I told him why. It was Good Friday. My mind was recalling Jesus' suffering and humiliation. The crown of thorns pushed in His head, being whipped and beaten, being stoned and spat upon as he carried the cross, and finally – being nailed to the cross. Whatever pain I was feeling was nothing compared to what Jesus suffered, and His day of torment got me through mine. Thank goodness for medical progress; the pneumoencephalogram was replaced by the painless CAT scan shortly after.

The hospital stay for the surgery was two weeks, and Mom drove up to take care of Bill, Billy, and Michele. She cooked all the meals, got her bargains at the supermarket, kept the house clean, helped the kids with their schoolwork, took them to Friendly's, and quietly filled our home with her never-ending love. The coffee pot was always brewing as she read her newspapers. The day before the surgery, I asked the doctor who would be with him around the operating table. (Mom always said, "Don't let some intern use you to practice on.") After he answered, I told him he forgot someone—Jesus. He said if I kept this stuff up, I'd end up converting him to Catholicism. I said, "Good! The church can use the money of a good Jewish doctor!" Bill and I felt very blessed that night when we got a phone call from our Marriage Encounter friends in New York offering their love, prayers, and support. Bill and I tried to be strong for each other, and Lorraine was softly crying as she and Erich got on the hospital elevator to leave. The next day, April 30, 1976, the successful surgery took place, and I awakened hearing the doctor saying, "It's benign." While in ICU I heard Mom quietly saying, "My baby. My baby. My beautiful baby," while gently holding my hand. I wanted to console her and say, "I'm okay," but I couldn't. Since the surgery was done through the mouth, the nose broken in the process, on the outside I looked like I had had a nose job. My lips were swollen and taut across my mouth, and when Billy saw me he said I looked like *Planet of the Apes. And I did!*

Once my pituitary gland was removed, the final part of the surgery involved making an incision in my inner thigh and removing some fat to replace the pea-sized gland. Dr. Gold said he'd try to make it as unobvious as possible, to avoid me embarrassment. He grinned when I responded, "Anyone that high up on my leg isn't worried about scars." As the incision was healing, I actually had two people ask me what it was from. You should have seen their faces when I answered, "Believe it or not, I had brain surgery." I walked away humming, "Let's give them something to talk about." The surgery was followed up with six weeks of precautionary radiation treatments. There was no follow-up medication, and I'm back to normal me again.

When I got home from the hospital, Dad came up by Greyhound bus for Mother's Day. He walked, *Sunday Times* in hand, a good mile from the bus stop, and showed up at our door happy and full of hugs and kisses—especially for Mom, who he missed a lot. We all sat down and feasted on Mom's delicious pot roast dinner. With easy access to the coffee pot, Mom and Dad always stayed in the guest room on the first floor and enjoyed sitting on the patio in the country air. There were trains within hearing distance, and Daddy loved the sound of them and the whistles blowing in the night. He said it reminded him of his childhood in Brooklyn.

After my surgery, Tommy drove up to Massachusetts in his brand-new Datsun. He slept on the living room couch, so he could see, hear, and be near his car. His baby! He worked hard for it, was proud of it, and took good care of his treasured purchase. I think if he could have found a way, he would have brought it into the living room and slept in it! Billy and Michele loved Tommy and were thrilled when he took them for a ride in his new car! We all enjoyed being together, but I think what Tommy liked most about visiting was his opportunity to speak with Bill about his plans for the future.

When Mom and Dad drove home, Dolores came up to fill in as I recuperated. I opened the door and there she stood—pretty as ever, holding an overnight bag. She looked like a blonde Mary Poppins, and I expected her to pull out a big floor lamp from her bag! Billy and Michele loved her, and we were all treated to her delicious cooking and fun-loving ways. Boy, were we blessed! Between Mom and Dolores we not only ate great, but there was also that "everything's going to be all right" feeling that enveloped all of us. In our prayers, we thanked God for each other and were grateful for family and the unending love and support they shared with us.

When things started getting back to normal, it became apparent to Bill and me how everything that happened was in God's Plan for us. Seeking an answer to an unknown problem, God in His wisdom reached out His hands and gently led us to Massachusetts to find the answer. Unbeknownst to us at the time,

He guided us in the right direction—meeting Dr. Fitz, who was sharp and called for the right X-rays and putting our trust in Dr. Gold, a fellow New Yorker with that helpful sense of humor and bantering, who performed the surgery via the mouth. (Any other neurosurgeon in Springfield would have drilled through the head.) My feeling God's presence during an extremely painful test on Good Friday. All was a blessing in disguise and a true faith experience. I have a whole new outlook on life since this fear of possible death occurred. I realize how little in life is *really* important. Who is there to impress? God and myself. What is *really* important in life? God, Bill, Billy, and Michele, and our life together as a family. My daily aim is to try to put a smile on someone's face—a compliment to a stranger, helping someone less fortunate, amusing strangers while in line in the supermarket, being aware of people and their needs, showing my "magic nose" to a crying toddler, telling a corny joke, and I'm sure to say "I love you" when hanging up the phone or saying good-bye to someone. Life is too short not to.

Bill and I bought a house in Hampden, Massachusetts, a small town just south of Springfield. It was an oversized cape with an above-ground pool, breezeway, and huge garage, and Mom and Dad asked if there was a hay loft! They loved visiting and stayed in their own room downstairs, near the bathroom and coffee pot! Grandma Wolf came with them once after her stroke and stayed with us for a week. She was doted upon and catered to by all of us, especially Billy and Michele. She always had bunions and loved having her feet massaged. Tommy came to visit us in his brand-new Porsche and again slept on the couch to be near his "baby." We probably should have hired a security guard to watch it so Tommy could get some sleep!

We then moved to the East Forest Park section of Springfield, about a mile away from Lorraine and Erich. It was within walking distance of Holy Cross Church and elementary school, and the well-reputed Cathedral High School, where our kids and Lorraine's kids went. Lorraine didn't drive, so I'd pick her up and we'd go to the school meetings together. Although sisters, we're like opposite ends of a pole. At the school meetings, I sometimes raised my hand to speak if I had a question. Lorraine would cringe and looked like she wanted to say, "I don't know her!" I sensed her discomfort, thought it was funny, and told her she didn't have to sit by me. At future meetings, she sat elsewhere. No biggie! Like Mom always said, "Each of us is unique."

Since Dad was only working at the *New York Times* now, Mom and Dad cherished their time together. They continued taking bus trips to Atlantic City, Canada, and everywhere. They flew to Las Vegas to see Elvis Presley, who Mom liked a lot. They were disappointed because Elvis was so overweight, seemed drunk or high, forgot the words to songs, and was on a downward trend. One of their trips was to Sarasota, Florida, where they made an absolutely fantastic purchase of time share units for the purpose of us brothers and sisters vacationing together in July and August—if we chose to. Some of us have purchased additional units, and for twenty-five-plus years we "Upton Kids" have spent a week or two with various siblings, each in our own unit, doing our own thing. Our children loved it, as do the grandchildren now! It's a beautiful resort on the aqua blue Gulf of Mexico, and we still enjoy the beach, pool, and palm-shaded surroundings—and being with family. It was an excellent, generous choice made by Mom and Dad.

They would take whatever grandkids fit in their car to amusement parks and for ice cream treats and somehow always managed to be there for birthdays, First Communions,

Confirmations, and graduations, no matter where they were held—New York, New Jersey, Massachusetts, Minneapolis, or Arizona. We used to kid that Grandma and Grandpa Upton *must have* had themselves cloned! Tommy and Adrianne loved to go up to Dolores and Don's and have fun with their "nieces and nephew." Adrianne, Doreen, and Denise had their own singing group—The Shamrocks—so entertainment was always available.

Sometimes Mom and Dad would show up unexpectedly in Massachusetts at Lorraine and Erich's or our house. Whatever good buys they had gotten on sale and given to our brothers and sisters in New York, they brought up to us also. Fair is fair! One time Mom came up with corned beef for Lorraine and I, because it was only 79¢ a pound. We told her it was on sale in Springfield for 69¢ a pound. Well, she hopped in the car, went to the store, and bought more corned beef for us and our New York brothers and sisters. Fair is fair! She was in her glory! After this, no one could believe a thing any of us Uptons said. We were obviously all full of *bull!*

A favorite place that Mom and Dad loved to go in Springfield was Gus and Paul's Bakery, a Jewish deli/bakery whose owners were originally from New York City. *Everybody* went there. I always bought Mom her favorite, creamed herring, which she loved. Bagels, Kosher delicacies, rolls, pastries, donuts, pies, cakes—you just wanted to taste and buy everything! Mom and Dad always bought a great variety of cakes and all sorts of goodies from Gus and Paul's for us and Lorraine and Erich and all the kids. When George and Peggy came up with the kids, a prime spot to visit was Friendly Ice Cream Shop. George delighted in treating all of us to our favorite three-scoop sundaes, which were only 99¢ then!

In 1978, Mom surprised all of us by announcing that she

went to school and got her GED. She was embarrassed for us to know she never graduated high school. Being so smart and on top of things, none of us ever suspected that Mom hadn't graduated. This woman who made education a top priority in our home went through life with this secret within—and did something about it! She certainly set an example for the younger generation about the importance of a degree. She felt accomplished and content earning her GED, and all of us were very proud of our Mom, once again.

In May of 1981, Don and Dolores had a surprise 45th anniversary party for Mom and Dad in their finished basement in Pearl River. All twelve of us were there. Nothing made them happier than to be surrounded by their children. Wearing a lovely corsage, Mom looked beautiful as she danced with Dad, who was still tall and handsome. Cameras were flashing all night, everyone laughing and clowning around. Tall, good-looking Tommy was 24, and Adrianne, the "baby," was now 20 and a lovely young lady. I look at the photos from that night and think, "Were we really ever so young?"

Mom & Dad's 45th anniversary – May, 1981
(bottom) George, Sr. and Elvira Upton
(center) Patty, Adrianne, Lorraine, Reenie, Dolores, Jeri
(top) Eddie, Raymond, Robert, Dennis, Tommy, George, Jr.

Chapter 20

During the summer that year—1981—Dolores and Don came out to stay a few days in the cottage we rented in Wellfleet, Cape Cod, for our family vacation. The cottage was set back on top of the dunes, overlooking the ocean. Days were spent riding the waves onto the shore and relaxing in the sun. Billy and Michele, who usually brought along a cousin or friend, loved it when we all stayed up late playing board games, eventually falling asleep to the sound of ocean waves lapping at the shore. We were close to Dolores and Don and always enjoyed each other's company. She and I talked every day on the phone, and I knew she was concerned about a consistent pain in her back, and no doctor seemed capable of finding its cause. Frustrated, Don suggested she go in the hospital and once and for all find the reason for the pain. Dolores went into NY University Hospital, and I went down to be with her. Don, who always seemed to know *someone everywhere*, had an ex-NYPD friend who worked in the parking lot and had a spot set aside for me. I went right up to see Dolores, who told me the doctors had just found the cause of the pain in her back. Dolores, who never smoked a cigarette in her life, was diagnosed with terminal lung cancer. I was dumbfounded but didn't cry because I didn't want to upset her.

Don and I talked in the lounge, and he asked me to stay while he told my parents, who were on their way to the hospital. Mom drove and got there first, and Don, in his most loving and gentle way, told Mom, who then went in to see Dolores. Dad took the train, and when he got off the elevator, Don and I were waiting in the lounge. My heart was aching for Don as he again found the words to tell my father. When finished, Dad stared out the lounge window and said, "Boy, it's raining like hell." He then went in to see Dolores, and Don was concerned that my father didn't understand what he'd told him. Knowing my father well, I assured Don that Dad heard and understood every word he said. His heart was breaking.

I stayed in Woodhaven with loving friends, Pat and Bob, and used their phone to call all my brothers and sisters to tell them the heart-rending diagnosis for Dolores and went back to visit her the next day. She looked as beautiful as ever and told me the doctors had been in to explain the radiation treatments and chemotherapy that would be taking place to deal with the cancer. We talked, we hugged, we laughed, we cried, and we prayed together. Ironically, in walked a man we both knew. Rubin, my father's friend from West Chemical, who was the photographer at both of our weddings, was a volunteer at the hospital and worked on the same floor Dolores was on. Dad was surprised and happy to see Rubin, who assured him he would take special care of Dolores.

I returned to Massachusetts, and Dolores and I spoke almost every day on the phone, as we always had. To be honest, it bothered me a great deal that some of my brothers and sisters didn't call Dolores and Don during her illness, because they felt uncomfortable and didn't know what to say. I never said anything to anyone but was disappointed and had a hard time accepting their lack of support. Dolores and I talked as usual about the kids, what events were coming up, what was on sale in the supermarkets, getting a haircut, looking for an outfit for something, and also the progress being made medically. The treatments were taking place. We visited them, and Don and Dolores visited us; life went on. I made a point of keeping all my brothers and sisters informed of Dolores' progress.

Before you knew it, Christmas was upon us! We made an annual habit of going to the Upton Christmas party, visiting Bill's family, and then staying in midtown Manhattan for a few days. Billy and Michele loved going to Mama Leone's, riding in a horse and buggy through Central Park, and just walking in the winter wonderland of Christmas displays. Since we moved to Massachusetts, Ray and Diane had the annual Upton Christmas party a few times at their house, and then Jeri had it at her house. Santa was there for all the kids, and new babies on his lap were the norm in our ever-growing family. Christmas 1981 was the year I bought the record "Daddy's Little Girl" by Al Martino for each of my brothers and brothers-in-law. It was played a few times that night, and I was so happy as the young fathers danced with their daughters. The most memorable and touching moment for me was to watch Daddy dance with his "Little Girls"—Dolores, Reenie, Jeri, Adrianne, and me—each held in the arms of this loving, hard-working, always happy man who was our father. (Lorraine wasn't there due to bad weather.) Although it was cold and wintry outside, the house was filled with the heart-warming love of family.

The year 1982 was welcomed by all of us, but as it progressed, it turned out to be a heart breaker. Bill's parents had retired and were living in Vero Beach, Florida. On June 5, Bill's dad died of a sudden heart attack and was waked and buried in New York. We vacationed in Wellfleet, Cape Cod, in July, and Dolores and Don joined us for a few days. Since she was taking different medications, Dolores had to carefully cover herself for protection against the sun. Relaxed and rested from the day at the beach, we all went for dinner and came back to the cottage and played cards or board games, laughing as Billy and Michele usually whooped us all!

Dolores and Don's 25th wedding anniversary was coming up in November, and a party was being planned. They decided to celebrate their anniversary early, and Labor Day weekend seemed the perfect time to get everybody together. Their daughter, Doreen, was working in Nicarauga for the Peace Corps and came home early due to her mom's illness. We Uptons all looked forward to getting together with Don's fun-loving twelve McGuire brothers and sisters! Shortly before the party took place, Daddy had a heart attack and was hospitalized but in no way was going to miss Don and Dolores's celebration on September 4. He said the doctor gave him permission to go, but I still think he signed himself out of the hospital. Dad looked pale and tired, but he was there in St. Margaret's church to see Dolores and Don renew their wedding vows. A big reception followed, and the Uptons and McGuires and all Don and Dolores' friends danced the night away. Don's sister Kathy was wearing the same dress as me, so I went over, gave her a big hug, and said it was nice knowing someone else who had excellent taste! At one point, Dad was quietly sitting at the table, looking very reflective, so I went over and asked him how he was feeling. He answered, "Patty, I danced with my daughter Dolores, I danced with your mother, I had a cigarette, and I had a high ball." His answer told me he was content to be with family and was aware and open to whatever lay ahead. Mom and Dad stayed overnight at Dolores and Don's, and Bill, Billy, Michele, and I stayed in a nearby hotel. On Sunday we stopped by to say good-bye to everyone and headed back to Massachusetts.

The next day—Monday, September 6, Labor Day—we got the devastating call that Dad had died of a massive heart attack at home. He was 70 years old. We immediately headed to New York to be with Mom, Tommy, and Adrianne and the whole family. George took care of the newspaper obituary and helped with the arrangements at Simonson's Funeral Home in Richmond Hill, which was up the street from where my father's Aunt Jen lived. She was the eldest Upton family member, was always treated with respect, but wasn't too well liked. She was a widow, never had children, had money, and always had a snooty way about her. As Lorraine and I were standing in front of the funeral home, Aunt Jen came right up to us and said, "It's your mother's fault. It's your mother's fault George is dead. He never should have gone to that party." I assured Aunt Jen that nothing pleased my father more than to be surrounded by his family and that it was his choice to be there. She huffed off and I followed her as she barged through the crowd and went right up to my mother's face and said, "Vera—it's your fault! It's your fault George is dead!" Mom was shocked, and I took her away as she cried from the hurtful remarks of a woman who never knew or understood what love was about. Upset as she was, Mom was consoled knowing there was nothing that was going to keep Daddy from going to Don and Dolores' anniversary celebration.

At the funeral home, I noticed a middle-aged black couple enter, looking kind of apprehensive. I approached them and said I was George's daughter Patty. The man said, "I know you're Patty. You're married to Bill, live in Massachusetts, and have two children, Billy and Michele." I was totally surprised and asked if we had ever met. He said no, and that he worked for years with my father at West Chemical, and that George talked all the time about his twelve children. I felt deeply touched and thanked him and his wife for coming to pay their respects. He continued speaking and told me he had deep respect for my father because Dad fought for him to get his union card—which he did—to work at the *New York Times*. I knew what he was saying; my father went to bat for a black man. I assured him that he must be a good, hard-working man if my dad did this. I then took them to meet Mom and in my heart thanked God for the fair-minded, just, and righteous man who was my father.

One of my sisters quietly told me it wasn't right for us to stay at Mom's house, because she should be allowed time alone with Tommy and Adrianne, who still lived at home. My instincts told me otherwise. Bill and I were very aware not to intrude in the time Mom spent talking with and consoling Tommy and Adrianne, who were totally devastated by their father's death. Mom was strong for them. (Don't we all try to hide our own hurt and be strong for each other at times like this?) Tommy and Adrianne went to bed, as did Bill, Billy, and Michele. Mom was alone, and she needed someone too. I was there to listen to and console her when she fell into my arms and cried how she would miss Daddy's arms around her, his sense of humor, jokes, and laughter—and even his snoring. She was heartbroken and grief stricken, thinking of life without her sweetheart George, and finally fell into a deep, much-needed sleep.

George made the arrangements to have the funeral Mass said by a priest friend of his at St. Bennies in Richmond Hill, which was where we all had childhood memories. The priest gave a very nice eulogy, but (I felt) he didn't really *know* Dad, or speak about the father we knew and loved. He spoke of Mr. Upton. He didn't speak of the happy-go-lucky Irishman George who, for over thirty years, undauntedly worked two full-time jobs and sacrificed and devoted his life to his wife Vera and the well being of their twelve children. I vowed to myself never to let this happen again. When it came time for communion, Mom felt uncomfortable because she was Lutheran. I reminded her of her own words—"there's only one God, and it's the same God"—and that Daddy would want her to. She received the sacrament with all of us. Dad was buried in Holy Rood Cemetery in Westbury, even though half of us, including the hearse, got lost along the way. Daddy was known to be late sometimes, and as George said that day, "Daddy was even late for his own funeral!" We all felt that Daddy's dying on Labor Day was almost a well-deserved tribute to a man whose life was spent unselfishly working so hard.

Jeri and her kids lived near Mom, and there was a mutual "keeping an eye out" for each other. Having Tommy and Adrianne at home was a big help to Mom. Tommy was working at a big computer company and doing very well. Adrianne had done some modeling, TV commercials, and even went to Hollywood and got a small role in a movie. She also worked for a travel agency, spending time at and rating different resorts. (Sounds like tough work, huh?) She dated different men but seemed to like this fellow John Mandelino. Once while I was visiting Mom's, Adrianne was sitting on the couch with her cream-covered arms and hands extended straight out, her legs raised and reaching outward with stuff all over her feet and toes, and her face was covered with all this white gook. She spoke through her teeth, barely moved her lips, and said, "I can't talk now. I'm doing a facial." When finished, she came to Mom's kitchen, looking like regular, pretty Adrianne, and I asked her what that stuff was that was all over her feet. She said she was doing a pedicure and was surprised I didn't know about or ever have one. Mom, drinking her coffee, sputtered when I said, "Adrianne, things have changed. When we were growing up, we were lucky we had shoes!"

Mom, never one to sit around doing nothing, was always on the go. Wherever she went shopping, the clerk would have to wait while Mom turned around and reached into her bra to get the money to pay. She didn't carry a pocketbook and always kept her money pinned in her bra for safe keeping. (I tried it once, but the money fell straight down!) Of course, while reaching into her bra, she had to be careful not to snag the money on the big wad of rubber bands that were always on her wrist. "You never know when somebody might need a rubber band." Having twelve children, through the years Mom and Dad had accumulated many gift certificates for various restaurants, and quite often Mom would take a slew of us out to dinner just to use them up. And of course Mom visited Dolores and Don in Pearl River, as it was obvious the cancer was taking its toll.

With Dolores' health in mind, celebrating their 25th wedding anniversary on Labor Day was a very wise choice. Bill and I visited Dolores and Don, and Dolores and I spoke every day with each other. She was still on chemotherapy, but we both knew what was happening. Dolores was in a hospice for a while, but chose to go home. Bill and I went to visit and brought Billy's high school graduation pictures to give to her. Dolores was Billy's Godmother, and she was happy to see how handsome he was. Her most loving husband Don then made phone calls to all the family, suggesting they come up to see Dolores, and those who could make it did. We were asked to stay but went home to Springfield. Mom stayed with Dolores, Don, Don Jr., Doreen, and Denise, and was there the next day on November 20, 1982, when Dolores passed away at age 44. Even though we all knew this would happen, it didn't make it any easier or hurt less.

I'm having a hard time writing this, because losing Dolores was the hardest death I ever had to deal with. Since Don worked for security at Yankee Stadium, flowers from the team and individual players came in abundance. Countless family and friends were there. Our Billy, 16, spent his first full paycheck on beautiful flowers for his much-loved Godmother, and his and Michele's favorite aunt. A bouquet to "Sister—Best Friend" was beside her, as were flowers from Mom, which were to, "My Baby." Mom's heart was filled with pain for the loss of her child. God in His mercy saved Daddy from this heartbreak. Dolores was buried on November 23rd, their 25th wedding anniversary. It was all so unfair. Why? Why this beautiful, loving couple with a great marriage, and three wonderful, loving, successful children who were raised so well? Why? Why my sister and friend? Why Dolores, who was loved, admired, and always there for everyone?

Boy was I mad at God! I remember riding in my car one day, hearing some news on the radio, and I couldn't wait to get home to call Dolores. Then it hit me. *She's gone!* And I pulled over and bawled my eyes out. For almost a year I searched within my soul to forgive God. I spoke with a priest, went to various prayer things at church, but nothing was giving me any sense of forgiveness or consolation. I even made a women's retreat (which is not my bag *at all*) at the Passionist Monastery. It started Friday night—*blah!* Saturday was a *drag*—and they sent us to our rooms about 10:00 PM. I couldn't sleep! It was 3:00 AM, and I looked around the room. It contained a bed, a dresser, a Bible, a crucifix, and a lamp. Suddenly I started laughing hysterically, because I realized that at age forty-one, *it was the first time in my life I ever had my own room!* At breakfast Sunday morning, we were given a choice of three workshops to attend. I chose the right one. With eyes closed in deep concentration, we were guided through different levels of thoughts, feelings, and occurrences in our lives, discarding the "trash" along the way. It cleansed me of the deep anger and hurt I was feeling and helped me to accept that Dolores was at peace. I was finally at peace with myself and God.

On New Year's Eve 1982, Bill and I and Mary and Eddie were at Lorraine and Erich's house "celebrating" in a very quiet, saddened atmosphere At midnight when the New Year rolled in, we said, "Good-bye and good riddance" to 1982. Mom came up to Massachusetts in January for my birthday; Michele and I went to Jeri's for a bridal shower, and Mom was also in Springfield in early June for Billy's high school graduation. Surprisingly, she wasn't there in June for Michele's and Karen Weiss's eighth grade graduations—*because Adrianne was getting married!*

Chapter 21

On June 19, 1983 (Adrianne's 23rd birthday), John Mandelino and Adrianne Upton were married in St. Catherine of Sienna Church in Franklin Square. Tommy walked the beautiful bride, his little sister and close friend, down the aisle to the waiting handsome groom. Mom looked so happy and elegant in her floral dress, which had a *red* (of course) sash draping down the front. Her favorite flowers, gardenias, were the finishing touch. Tommy danced with Adrianne when Daddy would have. Mom was on the dance floor all night doing what she loved—dancing and being with her family. Of course, she missed Daddy, but I reminded her that he was there, in all of us. The photographer did a great job of fitting us all in for a family picture. All my sisters and brothers looked so pretty and handsome surrounding Mom and the bride and groom, and were, I must say, a good-looking bunch!

The newlyweds lived in the second-floor apartment in Mom's house, and Tommy was in his room in the basement. Mom loved having John and Adrianne in the house but was careful not to interfere. John enjoyed talking to "Mrs. U," as he called her, and listening to her words of wisdom about life. John was a hard-working auto body repairman and was striving to buy his own auto body shop, which he eventually did. Since Bill was dating me when Adrianne was a baby, he used to kid John by saying, "You may be her husband, but I saw her naked before you did!"

Adrianne and John had a tendency to "spoil" Mom, which she pretended not to like. She loved it! Adrianne bought her clothes and outfits that looked great on her. If Mom was complimented on the new dress, slacks, top, jewelry, or jacket she was wearing, she'd whisper, "You know how much this *cost?*" Even though

Mom was feisty and outspoken about some things, she was shy by nature when it came to adorning herself. With Adrianne's encouragement, light reddish color was added to Mom's hair, which was styled, looked pretty, and made her feel good. We all told her to forget the cost, because she well deserved to be pampered with nice things. Adrianne was generous by nature, and since she and I wore the same size, I was the lucky recipient of what I call her "hand-me-*ups*." Besides size, even though there are eighteen years between us, Adrianne and I are a lot alike in varying ways and always have been.

Bill and I went down quite often to see Mom—if you could catch her home! We'd stop and see Jeri and the kids and always went to visit Grandma Wolf at Trump Pavilion. Sometimes she recognized us, sometimes she didn't, but that was okay. Her loss of memory was a Godsend, because she didn't know about Dad and Dolores' passing. Mom had boxes and boxes of old undated family photos, and she and I would stay up most of the night and go through them. Many of them were curled up and had that old, almost-bronze type of finish. I would put names and dates, many times approximate, on the back of them, and often needed Mom's help to tell me who was who—old friends, family members from Germany, and people I was too young to know. She was funny, and we had a lot of laughs. Mom denied that she had to wear glasses and would squint to identify the people in the pictures. She had a photo of three guys in army uniforms and had no idea who they were. I told her they were her brothers—Erich, Herb, and Howie—and she kept squinting, saying, "Are you sure?" An eight-by-ten Lincoln Studio picture of one of my brothers wearing a red velvet suit was incorrectly marked, "Dennis." I knew it was Raymond, and Mom asked if I was sure, because Dennis had his picture taken in the red velvet suit. I said, "Mom, *all* the boys had their pictures taken in the red velvet suit."

I enjoyed it so much being alone with Mom. She talked about her friends from when she lived in Manhattan and Brooklyn and said most of them were Jewish. We got to talking about religion, and Mom said she always believed the Jewish faith was the true one. I wasn't surprised, had heard it before, and said if she felt that way she should convert to Judaism. She said she didn't have to—her faith was in her heart. As we continued through the old pictures, different stories were relayed about the people in them, her childhood years, and hard times—like the Depression. Seeing the photos, I know for sure Mom was a beautiful young woman—a foxy lady, as our Billy said—dressed in the fashion of the day. I deeply enjoyed our special time together, and if you can understand, I felt I finally had the relationship with Mom that she was too busy for in my younger years.

One weekend I stayed at Mom's to attend a DC class reunion. I knew I'd be home early, so I told her to think about who she'd like to visit—no matter how far they lived—and I'd drive and we'd go there when I got home. I knew Mom didn't like to drive in the dark (she denied that, too). After the reunion, Mom decided to see Uncle Tom in Flatbush, but he wasn't home. Her next choice was Julia and Herb in Ozone Park, and off we went. I sat quietly as Mom and Julia talked a mile a minute about everything under the sun, including family. At one point, Julia told Mom that one of my cousins, the daughter of Mom's brother, wasn't really his child. Well, Mom's eyes almost bugged out of her head as she gave me a quick glance and motioned to Julia, "big ears." I didn't know if I should laugh or cry! Mom always used the term "big ears" if something was being talked about that nearby children or anyone shouldn't be privy to. For crying out loud, I was in my forties, and she was still worried about "big ears"?

When we got home that night, we labeled more pictures. We were making progress, but there were still many more. It was after midnight when Mom said she felt like having some Swiss cheese but didn't have any. I said no problem and quickly changed from my PJs into my jeans, and off we went to Shoprite. We got to the deli department, and Mom was relieved there was no crowd waiting. (At 1:00 AM?) She ordered the Swiss cheese but wanted to see it first, and then said, "Nah. It doesn't have enough holes." We left empty handed and went back to continue dating old pictures. God bless her, life with Mom was always an unexpected experience! Like the time she was upset that a recently born grandchild had not yet been christened. Unknown to the parents, Mom took it upon herself to baptize the baby in the kitchen sink. So now we have a *double Christian*—made Catholic by a Lutheran! A church baptism followed later.

It was about a year after Daddy died that I went to Mom's alone. I suggested that it was time to go through his clothes, reminding her that someone in need could use them. It was difficult for her, but she agreed. You can't even imagine all that there was. Besides the already worn clothing that was in the closets and drawers, there were piles of brand-new shirts, ties, handkerchiefs, sweaters, pants, belts, and jackets still in their original unopened packaging—accumulated gifts received by the father of twelve children. We went to the stores and got cardboard boxes, after Mom agreed to have them picked up by Goodwill on Monday. As we packed each box, Mom kept saying, "Oh, that shirt would look nice on Raymond." "George would like that." "That would be good for Eddie." "Dennis could wear that in Arizona." "Robert could use that." "That would be nice for Tommy." I gently reminded her that the boys all loved Daddy, but they didn't want or need his clothes. They could be used by men his age and be put to good use.

Then I came across the treasure of all treasures—a *great big* cardboard box filled with used shoelaces! Mom reached for it and said, "Oh, no—you're not touching that. You never know when someone needs a shoelace." She put her head down, feeling a little silly about what she said. I gently lifted her chin, looked in her eyes, and softly said, "Mom, when is the last time someone called you for a shoelace?" I told her if someone needed a shoelace, they'd buy it. She halfheartedly agreed to go through them and save only the good ones, which were put in a *much* smaller box. By Sunday morning, as I was preparing to leave, the living room was filled with cardboard boxes stacked on the floor and furniture, ready to be picked up by Goodwill the next day. Then Mom started poking through them, saying the boys could use this … or that. I went out to my car, opened the trunk and all the doors, and filled it with every box in the living room. I knew if I left them, they would still be there when I came back again. I called Goodwill, cancelled the pickup, and said I would give everything to a needy organization in Springfield. It certainly wasn't easy for Mom or me to go through Dad's stuff. My heart ached all the way home knowing treasured memories of Daddy were with me. I called Mom later in the week to say the clothes were deeply appreciated by an organization in Springfield that took care of older men in need.

Happily, the McGuire and Weiss families shared in the Stamm Thanksgiving feast, and before you knew it we were all gathered at Jeri's for the annual Christmas party! Fran, Manu, Tarun, and Juti were down from Canada to see Fran's mom and squeezed in at the Upton party too. They then came up to Springfield, and welcomed the New Year—1984—with Bill and I, Lorraine and Erich, and Mary and Eddie. Mom came up in January—in her red outfit—for my 42nd birthday. She ventured by herself many times to the Stamm or Weiss home in Springfield for all occasions—birthdays, Communions, Confirmations, graduations—as she did for all her other children and grandchildren. She even came up when Michele was in Cathedral High School's Minstrel show. At one point, a singer came on stage in an eye-catching fitted red gown, and Mom whispered, "Wow! Look at that one in the red dress!" And I whispered back, "Mom, that's your granddaughter."

The weddings weren't over yet! On Friday, August 24, 1984, Thomas Upton and Angela were married at St. Anthony of Padua Church in East Northport, followed by a satiating reception at the Larkfield Manor. Being it was a Friday night, the cocktail hour and buffet assortments were enough to satisfy anyone's hunger—and then we went into the main dining room for dinner! We started off with lemon sherbet to "cleanse our palate" (which we didn't even know we had, or that it was dirty!). Six-foot-five Tommy had to lean over a bit to dance with 5'2" Mom, who looked so elegant in her favorite red dress with black sequins. She got very upset to see the waiters clearing the tables and throwing away the shrimp, prime rib, and chicken dinners that weren't finished. She was close to tears pleading with the waiters to give it to the poor and hungry. We understood how she felt seeing food wasted but also knew it was against the law to give it away. Everybody was well fed, and all proceeded with the dancing and festivities of the night and had a great time! Tommy and Angela were on the path to a lifetime of wedded bliss!

The annual Upton Christmas party was at Ray and Diane's house, and Santa George did a good job of distributing gifts from the North Pole. Tommy and Angela were expecting in the spring, but Mom drove Angela to the hospital unexpectedly early in very icy, treacherous conditions. Thomas Upton Jr. was born prematurely on February 14, weighing only two pounds. He was so tiny but survived against all odds with excellent preemie care. He was dubbed the "miracle baby" at the hospital and today is a strapping six-footer. He became a big brother to Justin after Tommy and Angela moved into a brand-new home in Mt. Sinai.

In March 1985, the Uptons, McGuires, and a lot of Pearl River, New York, residents gathered to celebrate and welcome home Denise McGuire from Calcutta, India, where she had worked with Mother Teresa since shortly after her mother's passing. We have postcards from Denise while she was in India, and they are mind-boggling to read. When she first met Mother Teresa she was wearing a new, simple T-shirt, and Mother Teresa asked her how much she paid for it, to which Denise responded, "$5." Mother Teresa said, "You should have paid $2 and given the rest to the poor." There was no union, no pay, and squalid living conditions in exchange for sharing Jesus' love and compassion for the poor and needy. The joyous feelings of thankful family and friends filled the air as Denise was welcomed home.

Shortly afterward, Mom came to Springfield, and we took her to Hartford, Connecticut, to see Mickey Rooney and Anne Miller live. She absolutely enjoyed the hilarious jokes and antics of Mickey Rooney and couldn't get over how Anne Miller could still dance and kick her long legs. We were all totally entertained by these two unforgettable characters. Mom said Dad would have liked seeing these two old timers. Bus trips with Dad were sorely missed by Mom, but Reenie and Adrianne accompanied her to Atlantic City, New England, or Canada once in a while.

Whenever we visited Mom or she came to Springfield, she and

Bill would talk for hours about the stock market, investments, real estate, sounding like two Wall-Street know-it-alls. Talk is cheap, it didn't cost them a cent, and they both enjoyed it! I usually found these conversations kind of boring and didn't participate. Over coffee in Springfield one night, Mom said she had something very important to tell me. It was a secret, and I was to tell *no one!* She confided in me that she had decided to have my husband Bill as executor of her will. I said fine, but *no way* was it going to be kept a secret! I reminded her that George, as the eldest, expected to be the executor, and if something happened to her, the family would be shocked and George would be hurt if Bill popped up out of the blue and said, "I am." I had no objections to Bill being executor but wanted her to see the confusion it would cause if it were kept secret. Mom understood and agreed to tell all my brothers and sisters of her decision, which she did.

Mom was always a well-organized person, and it was quite obvious she was "getting her house in order" in preparation for her eventual demise. She and I went through tons of pictures. They were broken down into twelve family packets, and Mom gave each of her sons and daughters their family photo memories. Mom specified she wanted Eddie and me, both music lovers, to have her records. She also said that she wanted her body donated to science. For years she used to say what a waste of money funerals were, and tell us, "When I go, just put me in an orange crate and bury me in the yard!" She thought possibly her skin could be used for burn victims, her eyes could be used by someone, and her body could give scientific clues to the results of TB. She was also content knowing that everyone was settled. Grandma Wolf was still in Trump Pavilion being well taken care of and visited often by the family; Adrianne and John were happy and doing well; Tommy and Angela were settled in Mt. Sinai; Robert was married and bought a house in New Jersey and had a daughter, Darlene; Jeri and the kids were doing well; and Don McGuire, whom she loved like a son, was engaged to a very lovely woman. Life was falling into place. But that didn't slow her down or stop her from driving everywhere to see everybody and taking her bus trips!

Chapter 22

In September 1986, Mom asked me if I'd like to take a bus/cruise trip to Nova Scotia with her and Reenie and Adrianne, which sounded great. The bus left Long Island but had to sidetrack to pick me up in Hartford, Connecticut. As soon as I got to the top of the bus stairs, I announced to all the grey-haired riders, "Believe me, you'll never regret having made this stop!" With that Adrianne popped up in the back and said, "I knew it! I knew she couldn't get on the bus without saying something!" The Upton foursome was on its way—two peas in a pod and two nuts in a shell! We proceeded to the Sheraton Hotel in Maine where free coffee and donuts awaited us before our overnight cruise. To kill time, we went into the lounge instead to have coffee and dessert. Mom totally objected and wouldn't order a thing. She couldn't see wasting money when the donuts (which were down to crumbs) and coffee in the lobby were free. Adrianne was upset and begging her to order something, Reenie quietly shrugged her shoulders a few times, and I felt Mom was being childish and wouldn't give in to her stubbornness. We got our desserts, which Mom was silently eyeing, and finally she gave in and had some. (Sounds like a thick-headed German, eh?!) Then the bus got on the ship, and off we sailed into the night. The room on board was a little bit bigger than a small closet! Thankfully, none of us was overweight! The four beds were hooked on the wall—two on each side, upper and lower—with a very narrow space between. To put on deodorant, I suggested we use one deodorant, stand one behind the other and the person up front hold it and say, "Okay, ladies, left arm … now right arm" to apply it. There was a community bathroom down the hall. Mom was leery and insisted on covering the toilet seats with newspapers. "Bottom line"—–by the end of the cruise we were all well-read!

Once the ship passed the three-mile limit to Canada, the casinos were opened for betting. I was shocked to see Reenie and Adrianne dropping tens and twenties like pennies at the gambling tables. I'm too cheap not to get something for my money, so Mom and I spent our time at the nickel slots. To sleep, all we had to do was unhook our beds—a slab of wood with a thin mattress—from the wall. Adrianne and I got the top bunks. Our room was so low in the ship that you could see and hear the water splashing up against the porthole. (I was hoping there were oars and an inflatable raft in the room, just in case.) I couldn't sleep and asked if anyone wanted to tell ghost stories, but all I heard were a few grunts. I think Reenie was praying, because she said, "Oh God, here she goes again!" The next morning the bus rolled off the ship, and we stopped at a very nice restaurant for breakfast (all meals included) and spent the day riding around Nova Scotia. We stopped at every church along the way, and any time another tour bus pulled next to us in the parking lot, Mom would say, "Boy, I'm glad I'm not on that bus—there's nothing but old people." (Believe me, we were not on the Spring Chicken Express!)

We stopped for lunch and dinner along the way, and each time we did Mom continued a habit she always had—taking all the jelly packets on the table and stuffing them in her bag! Adrianne, who was carrying Mom's bag, said it was getting too heavy from the jellies, and if she didn't stop taking them she was going to report Mom to the restaurant manager! After genuflecting and kneeling all day in the many churches we stopped at, we were tired and finally got to the hotel. Adrianne walked into the big, spacious hotel room and literally fell on her knees, raising her hands in praise, saying, "Thank you, God! Thank you, God! Finally some room! With a real bed! And a bathroom with a shower! Thank you, God!" We all laughed but were also thankful for some room to spread out a bit. (Obviously this trip was humbling all of us to appreciate the everyday things we took for granted!)

The next morning we had to be up early for breakfast before leaving to continue the bus tour. Well, here's where the different personalities really came into play! Mom and Reenie were never ones to fuss. With a comb, they did one sweep to the left, then one sweep to the right, and they were ready. Adrianne and I did the hair curling, hairdo, hairspray, makeup, and the earrings, of course. Mom and Reenie (two peas in a pod) were sitting there staring with glum faces at us (two nuts in a shell). We told them to go ahead to breakfast and we'd catch up, and they finally did. We then bussed through the scenic countryside and had lunch along the way. (By popular demand, Vera was all jellied out!) We arrived at the pier to take the ship back but first had to be cleared through Canadian customs. Well, you had to be there!

The man from Customs got on the bus, stood by the driver, and gave a general: "Does anyone have drugs? Does anyone have any illegal substances? Are you all American citizens? Blah, blah, blah," to which all the passengers in unison responded yes or no. Two minutes later the Customs man came back on board and said, "Adrianne Mandelino and Patricia Stamm are to leave the bus and come with me." Adrianne looked like somebody shot her! She fell back in the seat, eyes bugging out of her head, exclaiming, "Why us? Why do they want us?" I kiddingly said, "Oh, Adrianne, it's those damn drugs." She got up, still saying, "Why us?" as we hurried down the aisle, and I said, "Adrianne, because we're the only ones young enough to get off the bus quick!"

Outside the bus there was a long table, surrounded by security guards, and our luggage was laying on it. The Customs man started to open Adrianne's suitcase, and she slammed her hand down on top of it and started reading him the riot act: "I'll sue you if you expose my personal garments, etc." Standing there bored silly, I partially lifted the lid on my suitcase and whispered into it, "It'll all be over in a few minutes, Bill." During all this, everyone on the bus was cramming on one side to see what was going on, taking pictures, and laughing their heads off. I thought the bus would tip over. We were cleared to leave Canada, and I have a feeling they were glad to see us go. The bus stopped for lunch in a Hartford restaurant where Bill was picking me up. He was happy to see us and asked how the tour went. We all agreed it was a nice trip and that we really enjoyed it. But I added, "Let's be honest. One more day together and one of us would be dead or seriously injured!"

With Mom in a pretty red outfit, at Christmas we all gathered at Jeri's for the ever-growing annual party. Three days later—December 28, 1986—Don McGuire married his lovely bride, Celeste! Mom, Jeri, Bill, and I were so happy to attend to see Don and Celeste looking so happy and in love. Seeing all the McGuires again was an added treat! With a mother's love, Mom's heart was filled with joy and contentment for the newlyweds.

Chapter 23

But as life goes, Mom was having some cardiac problems that were scheduled to be tended to in the New Year. Never one to complain, Mom knew there was evidence of some aortic blockage, and a balloon test was scheduled to see how the problem could be dealt with. I drove from Massachusetts early morning on February 6 and got to Northshore University Hospital, Manhasset, about 8:00 AM to be with Mom. We talked as we walked around the hospital floor, and she said she was open to whatever results the test would show. She was very much at ease and prepared. The nurses then readied Mom and put her on a gurney, and we were waiting by the elevator when Adrianne got off one, just in time to see Mom before the procedure. Kisses and I love yous were exchanged. Adrianne and I then went into the lounge to wait.

I noticed Mom's room being cleared out of all her belongings, but I didn't say anything to Adrianne. I just moseyed down to the nurses' station to inquire. They said she would be going to another room after the procedure. Just then the doctor, covered with blood, got off the elevator and explained that Mom's arteries were very hard and brittle, and hemorrhaging had occurred. What should he do? I simply told him to do whatever was necessary to save her. Adrianne saw the doctor, leaned back with outstretched arms against the wall, and said, "It's the 6th - just like Daddy died on the 6th!" I held her and assured her the doctors were trying their best. She and John were planning on starting a family, and she said, "Mommy will never see my babies!" I told her that if anything happened, Mommy would see her babies first from heaven. Fearful myself, I was trying very hard to be strong for Adrianne. We were then told to go down to the recovery room where Mom was. Oddly enough, Reenie and Jeri were just getting off the elevator, so the four of us went down together.

To me the place we went to was eerie and creepy, not like a regular recovery area, and I had a very foreboding feeling. We were quietly waiting for a short while, when a code blue was called, and medical personnel came running from all directions. We were hoping it wasn't for Mom. Sad to say, it was. The nurse then came out and told us Mom had died and asked immediately about organ donations. I told her she was leaving her body to science and thought her eyes might be of use to someone, or her skin for a burn victim. On February 6, 1987, our Mom, Elvira Upton, died of acute cardiac failure at the age of 72. As she requested, Mom was then sent to Stony Brook University School of Medicine/Anatomical Science.

We went to Jeri's, and I called Bill. He knew all of Mom's wishes and told me what to do before he came down. Adrianne and I made the arrangements at Simonson's Funeral Home, put together the newspaper obituary notice, and stopped at George's. I asked him if he wanted to go with us to Redeemer Lutheran Church in Glendale, which is where Mom received her sacraments as a child and where she wanted the service to be held. George was very upset about Mom's death, and I held him and reminded him how much Mommy loved him, her firstborn. Adrianne and I proceeded to Redeemer Lutheran Church, where the young pastor said we could not have the service there, because Mom was not an active member of the congregation. Adrianne got very upset and said, "You call yourself a Christian?" I quietly reminded her, which she wasn't really too aware of, of all the nonsense Mommy had taken from the Catholic Christians through the years. We left and called Uncle Herb and Aunt Julia to see if the service could be held at St. Matthew's in Ozone Park, where they and Grandma

Wolf had worshipped for years. Without question, Pastor Urdahl made the arrangements. The Lord was guiding us again.

In part, Mom's obituary notice read, "We wish to rejoice in our hearts for the fullness of life and the gift of love so generously shared with all of her children and recognize the compassionate way she touched the lives of so many others." Mom had requested, in lieu of flowers, that donations be made to St. Vincent de Paul Society at St. Benedict Joseph Labre. *She never forgot!* The funeral home was packed with family and friends, some looking puzzled, not knowing that Mom left her body to science. There was memorabilia from her children and grandchildren throughout the room. The funeral director told Bill that people attending other wakes kept asking him why there were so many people in that big room for Elvira Upton when there was no body. We went back to Mom's house, and I stayed up all night writing a eulogy, as I had vowed to do.

Pastor Urdahl was a very gentle, truly Christian man, who we all agreed looked like Ben Franklin. His hair was slightly longer, thinning on top, and he wore half-glasses, which were perched low on his nose. The service for Mom took place during an icy, treacherous snowstorm, and Pastor Urdahl warmly welcomed all of us snow-covered Catholics, including our cousin Jackie Upton and his wife Gladys, into St. Matthew's. Aunt Julia and Uncle Herb were the only Lutherans there. Pastor Urdahl patiently delayed the service as we all anxiously awaited the arrival of Tommy and Angela, who had a long and dangerous drive from Mt. Sinai, and Eddie and Mary, who slipped and skidded most of the way. Once started, it was so good to hear him speak lovingly of Vera, a woman he saw many times while visiting Grandma Wolf at Trump Memorial. He graciously allowed me to speak, and I determinedly recalled a lot of treasured memories of Mom.

If anyone had not yet cried, they did then. To again fulfill her wishes, we all went to dinner at Koenig's German Restaurant in Floral Park to gather as family.

There was an undeniably deep love and mutual respect for each other between Bill and Mom, and Bill worked earnestly to fulfill any and all of her wishes. Being a very organized man, any assets were distributed fairly and quickly. I did not participate in or have any knowledge of Mom's finances. (Ya know—big ears!) Bill handled everything according to Mom's will and wishes and did one heck of a superlative job. The love and respect shown by all my brothers and sisters was well appreciated. Bill even added some fun to the process! A list was made of the many unspecified odds and ends that belonged to Mom. He sent the list to each of us, with the understanding that whoever wanted something on the list had to make their choices, mark them, and send it *right back* in order to get first pickin's. The race was on! Then everyone gathered at Mom's house to see who the first-return designated winner was—Raymond—and anything unclaimed was put in a bag and passed around grab-bag style until all was gone! It was a fun time!

Adrianne and John bought Mom's house for fair market value, and they were blessed on March 15, 1988, with the birth of their beautiful daughter—dark-haired, brown-eyed Melissa Mandelino. I know Mom and Dad were smiling down from heaven. Three and a half years later Melissa was a big sister to her handsome brother, John Mandelino III. The only thing left to deal with in Mom's estate was Stony Brook University, which was where her body went. The agreement with them was for a year, but Bill received a call asking if they could keep Mom's remains longer, to which he said yes. Then one day Bill called from work to tell me a package was coming special delivery. I asked him what he ordered, to which he responded that the package was from Stony Brook University. Silence. The doorbell rang; I opened the door, signed for the package, and stood in the hall holding Mom's ashes. I quietly greeted her and said, "Now where should I put you, Mom?" Simple! I went right into the kitchen and put the package next to the coffee pot and can of coffee on the countertop! I wanted Mom to feel right at home!

Bill made arrangements at Holy Rood Cemetery to have Mom's ashes buried with Dad. He patiently and with loving care covered the metal container holding Mom's ashes with a list of names on each side—in memory of Dad, the children, the grandchildren, and the great-grandchildren. Bill had Mom's name inscribed under Dad's on the tombstone before the burial took place. He then arranged for a catered picnic to be held after the burial at Eisenhower Park, right across the street from Holy Rood Cemetery. At the burial site, Bill led everyone in prayer and asked if anyone would like to share their thoughts and feelings, to which some responded yes. The ashes were laid to rest at the foot of the tombstone of George and Elvira Upton and tended to by the cemetery workmen. Mom and Dad were at peace—and together again—on June 28, 1989, their wedding anniversary.

We all then went to Eisenhower Park and had one heck of a fun day! Eddie's wife, Mary, brought all the paraphernalia for potato-sack races, three-legged races, and face painting for the kids. Of course there were more than enough people for a riotous baseball game or two. All the grandchildren had a blast! Hot dogs, hamburgers, chicken, sausages, ice cream, watermelon, and all sorts of goodies kept everyone well nourished for the day's events.

It was a day that started out with feelings of loss and sadness and ended with the joy of being together as the family of George and Elvira Upton. I know Mom and Dad were with us that day—as they are to this day—in their "Legacy of Love."

UPDATE:

Grandma Wolf passed away on January 16, 1989 at the age of 98.

George and Peg Upton have thirteen grandchildren. Sadly, their son Kenneth passed away in June 2003.

Don and Celeste McGuire are grandparents to ten.

Bill and Pat Stamm live on Long Island and are grandparents to five.

Tom and Reenie Leak have twelve grandchildren.

Jeri Kline has five grandchildren. Sad to say, her oldest son, Daniel Jr., passed away April 24, 2008.

Erich and Lorraine Weiss have five grandchildren. Sadly, Erich Jr. passed away December 31, 2008.

Ray and Diane Upton are grandparents to four.

Edward Upton is engaged to be married, and the grandfather of one.

Dennis Upton is married to Debbie and has one grandchild.

Robert Upton is married to Geralynne and has no grandchildren.

Tommy and Angela Upton are busy with their ice hockey and golf-loving sons.

Adrianne Upton is divorced.

PS. Most of us have at least two or three bathrooms!

The annual Upton Christmas party has been held at a centrally located firehouse for about twenty years.

www.ingramcontent.com/pod-product-compliance
Ingram Content Group UK Ltd.
Pitfield, Milton Keynes, MK11 3LW, UK
UKHW041847190726
13854UKWH00002B/765